20th Century
Decorative British Tiles

Craft & Studio Tile Makers

Chris Blanchett

Schiffer Publishing Ltd

4880 Lower Valley Road, Atglen, PA 19310 USA

Dedication

This book is dedicated to Ken Beaulah who sowed the seed and
Kenneth Clark who watered it.

Other Schiffer Books by Chris Blanchett
20th Century Decorative British Tiles: Commercial Manufacturers, A-H
20th Century Decorative British Tiles: Commercial Manufacturers, J-W

Other Schiffer Books on Related Subjects
Art Nouveau Tiles, c. 1890-1914, by Sandie Fowler and Wendy Harvey
*The Encyclopedia of American Art Tiles: Region 1 New England States;
Region 2 Mid-Atlantic States,* by Norman Karlson
The Encyclopedia of American Art Tiles: Region 3 Midwestern States,
by Norman Karlson

*The Encyclopedia of American Art Tiles: Region 4 South and South-
western States; Region 5 Northwest and Northern California,* by
Norman Karlson
The Encyclopedia of American Art Tiles: Region 6 Southern California,
by Norman Karlson
California Tile: The Golden Era, 1910-1940: Acme to Handcraft, by
the California Heritage Museum
*California Tile: The Golden Era, 1910-1940: Hispano-Moresque to
Woolenius,* by the California Heritage Museum
Flint Faience Tiles A-Z, by Margaret Carney and Ken Galvas

Library of Congress Cataloging-in-Publication Data

Blanchett, Chris.
 20th century decorative British tiles craft & studio tile makers /
Chris Blanchett.
  p. cm.
 ISBN 0-7643-2468-3 (hardcover)
 1. Tiles—Great Britain—History—20th century. I. Title.

NK4670.7.G7B55 2006
738.60941'0904—dc22

                                    2006003652

Designed by Mark David Bowyer
Type set in Zapf Calligraphy BT / Adobe Jensen Pro BT

ISBN: 0-7643-2468-3
Printed in China
1 2 3 4

Published by Schiffer Publishing Ltd.
4880 Lower Valley Road
Atglen, PA 19310
Phone: (610) 593-1777; Fax: (610) 593-2002
E-mail: Info@schifferbooks.com

For the largest selection of fine reference books on this and related
subjects, please visit our web site at **www.schifferbooks.com**
We are always looking for people to write books on new and related
subjects. If you have an idea for a book please contact us at the
above address.

This book may be purchased from the publisher.
Include $3.95 for shipping.
Please try your bookstore first.
You may write for a free catalog.

In Europe, Schiffer books are distributed by
Bushwood Books
6 Marksbury Ave.
Kew Gardens
Surrey TW9 4JF England
Phone: 44 (0) 20 8392-8585; Fax: 44 (0) 20 8392-9876
E-mail: info@bushwoodbooks.co.uk
Website: www.bushwoodbooks.co.uk
Free postage in the U.K., Europe; air mail at cost.

Contents

Acknowledgments

This book, and the accompanying volumes on commercial tile makers, have taken three years to complete. They would not have been possible without the constant help and support of my wife, Julie, who has typed, corrected, retyped, and above all, encouraged. It would have taken even longer if she hadn't cracked the whip now and then!

I must also thank all the museums, collectors and tile makers who have so generously supplied information and photographs or let me photograph items that are missing from my own collection; the book would not have been anywhere near as complete without their contributions: Aldershaw Handmade Tiles Ltd. (Anthony Kindell), Mary Bentley, Maggie Angus Berkowitz, Julia Blanchett, Susanna Long, Michael Blood, The British Museum (Judy Rudoe), Caroline Campbell, Graham and Kim Carnduff-Young, Jon Catleugh, Kenneth and Ann Clark, Peter and Diana Clegg, Zena Corrigan, Chris and Michelle Cox, Craig Bragdy Design Ltd. (Jean Powell), Peter Creffield, Mr. and Mrs. Dick, Bryan Fahey, Malcolm Fletcher, May Gillespie, The Gladstone Pottery Museum, Stoke-on-Trent (Angela Lee), Adrian Grater, Ulrich Hamburg (Germany), Roger Hensman, Paul Henry, Highland Stoneware, Willem Irik, The Ironbridge Gorge Museum Trust (Michael Vanns), Jackfield Conservation (Lesley Durbin), Tony Johnson, Dorothy Mindenhall (Canada), Linette O'Sullivan, Paul and Angela Pitkin, The Potteries Museum & Art Gallery, Stoke-on-Trent, Shaws of Darwen (Jon Wilson), Thelma Shepley, Michael Spender, Carl Rosen, Rye Tiles Ltd. (Tarquin & Biddy Cole), Angela Sherborne, Pat and Joyce Smith, Freddie and Annie Taggart, Mark Tanner (www.antiquecalendar.com/tiles), Douglas van der Horst (South Africa), Hans van Lemmen, Peter Vincent, The Williamson Museum & Art Gallery, Birkenhead, Carolyn Wraight.

All photographs are by the author unless otherwise stated. I have tried to acknowledge all sources, but if I have omitted any, I apologize. Please let me know and I will rectify this in future editions. Please let me know if you find any omissions or errors too—I'm not too old to learn and things can be rectified or added in a later edition.

Introduction

The first two volumes in this series explore the work of commercial tile manufacturers, whilst this third volume concentrates on craft and studio potteries making tiles during the 20th century. Although these too can be said to be commercial, they were not large-scale producers; in fact, for many of them tiles were merely a sideline. That doesn't mean to say that their products are in any way inferior to those of commercial companies; the opposite is quite often true. Design is frequently the most important aspect of such tiles, rather than the expediencies of mass production. Craft and studio potters have the time and ability to use techniques that would be too expensive or time-consuming for commercial production, such as hand painting and sgraffito. They also have the ability to cope with a whole set of different problems, and are often working on commission—having to take the client's wishes into consideration.

Although I have tried to compile a comprehensive selection of craft and studio tiles, this is not a complete guide, nor could it ever be so. I still frequently come across tiles whose identity I have not been able to trace: in some cases potteries made only a handful of tiles, perhaps for the potter's own use. I have endeavored to include all the tiles that a collector is likely to find on his or her travels, along with a comprehensive collection of marks and characteristic designs, I hope it will help to enable the identification of many hitherto anonymous tile makers.

If you find any glaring omissions or errors, then please do not hesitate to contact me via the publisher—a second edition will provide the opportunity to right wrongs and fill gaps.

—Chris Blanchett

Notes

Unless otherwise stated, all tiles are dust-pressed, with the exception of encaustic tiles where the method of manufacture is always mentioned. Most dimensions are given in inches, as this is how they were originally quoted—the actual size may vary between individual tiles. Tiles that were made specifically in metric sizes are quoted in millimeters. The height of a tile always precedes the width, and all dimensions are approximate. The mention of a company name in *italics* indicates that they have their own entry elsewhere. (For commercial manufacturers, these entries will be found in the companion volumes to this book covering those manufacturers.) The same applies in the Glossary. In the captions, "Unknown commercial blank" indicates that the back of the tile is not visible because it is framed or stuck to a wall etc. "Unidentified commercial blank" indicates that the back of the tile can be seen but has so far eluded attribution.

Prices

Most of the tiles illustrated have a price group shown in the following format:

Price group A = £5.00 to £20.00 ($10.00 to $35.00)
Price group B = £20.00 to £50.00 ($35.00 to $85.00)
Price group C = £50.00 to £100.00 ($85.00 to $170.00)
Price group D = £100.00 to £200.00 ($170.00 to $350.00)
Price group E = £200.00 to £400.00 ($350.00 to $700.00)

Price group F = £400.00 to £1000.00 ($700.00 - $1750.00)
Price group G = over £1000.00 (over $1750.00)

Prices are quoted for tiles in very good condition, not necessarily as shown in the illustrations. Tiles with damage or faults will be worth considerably less. Prices are based on the author's experience in the British market—prices in the U.S.A. may vary substantially.

Glossary

Aerograph. A small, precise spray gun mainly used with *stencils* to create patterns on tiles and other materials. The nozzle can be adjusted to give a solid dense spray or a fine mist that can be used for shading.

Art Deco. An art and architecture movement of the 1920s and 1930s, noted for its bold geometric patterns and colors. The style is also sometimes referred to as "Moderne."

Art Nouveau. An art and architecture movement established in the mid-1890s, noted for its use of sinuous design elements, often incorporating stylized floral or figurative motifs. It was named after l'Art Nouveau, a shop in Paris, France that first promoted the style.

Barbotine. Using pigmented *slip* clays to paint a design on a tile (or other) surface. The design is painted over many times to create a raised effect on the tile surface. (See also: *Pâte-sur-Pâte*)

Biscuit. A tile that has been *biscuit-fired*, before any decoration or *glaze* has been applied.

Biscuit-Firing. The first *firing* that hardens the *body* ready for decoration and/or *glazing*.

Block Printing. A form of lithographic printing. The German engraver Aloys Senefelder (1771–1834) invented lithography in 1798. The printing surface is a smooth stone block with the printing and nonprinting areas being made grease-receptive and grease-repellent respectively. Greasy ink is then rolled over the entire area and is taken up only by the grease-receptive areas. Paper is then pressed onto the stone and the ink transfers to the paper, which is then applied to the tile front. (See also: *Collins and Reynolds Patent; Transfer-printing*)

Blunger. A large vat with rotating paddles used to mix clays and water to produce *slip*.

Body. A mixture of *clays* formulated for a specific purpose, i.e. color, texture or frost resistance etc.

Bottle Kiln. A traditional brick-built *kiln* whose shape resembles a large squat bottle.

Ceramic Colors. Pigments that are able to withstand the *firing* temperature of ceramics, i.e. in excess of 1000° Celsius.

Clay. A natural material (mainly alumina silicate) formed from the weathering and decomposition of rocks. It is found in most parts of the world and in many different colors due to contamination with various other materials such as iron.

It is easily shaped and holds its shape well, once dried. The shape becomes permanent when the clay is fired. (See also *Plastic Clay* and *Dust Clay*)

Cloisonné. The Dutch term for *Cuenca*.

Cobalt Blue. A rich, deep blue *ceramic color* produced from compounds of the metallic element cobalt, much used in the Far East and on Dutch and English *delftwares*. The main source is *Zaffer*, a cobalt ore found widely in the Middle East.

Collins and Reynolds Patent. A patent method of *block printing* onto tile surfaces that was much used by Herbert Minton, who bought the rights to the patent in 1848. Minton referred to the technique as the New Press process and produced many different series of picture tiles by this method, as well as geometric and floral patterns.

Cuenca. From the Spanish meaning "bowl." The term is used for tiles that have raised lines molded onto the surface to prevent different colored *glazes* running together in the firing. (See also *Cloisonné*)

Cuerda Seca. From the Spanish meaning "dry cord." In its earliest form, a thin cord impregnated with a waxy substance was laid in a pattern on the surface of the tile to contain and separate different colored *glazes*. Later, the line was drawn or printed on the surface of the tile with a waxy substance containing *manganese* pigment. The resultant tiles have a distinctive sunken matt black line surrounding each color in the pattern.

Crazing. Minor "fracturing" of the *glaze* surface due to one of a number of reasons: differing shrinkage rates of *biscuit* and *glaze* in the *glost firing*, absorption of moisture causing the tile body to swell, or slight flexing of the tile after installation. The presence of dissolved salts in moisture absorbed from the wall or floor on which the tiles are fixed can, in extreme cases, cause the glaze to flake off completely.

Crackle Glaze/Crackelure. The deliberate use of additives in the *glaze* designed to re-create the effects of *crazing*. Often used to create a false impression of age.

Delftware. A term applied to *tin-glazed earthenwares*, mainly from the Netherlands and Great Britain, generally decorated with *cobalt blue* or *manganese purple* pigments. Named after the Dutch town of Delft, a major centre for its production from the 17th century to the present day.

Dust Clay. Clay that has been dried to approximately 8% moisture content, creating a damp powder that can be easily formed by *dust-pressing*. Drying was originally done in a filter-press where the wet clay was placed in large filter bags and squeezed dry, the water escaping through the bag material. In more recent times, the clay is spray-dried by pumping through a nozzle past a stream of very hot air, causing the moisture to evaporate rapidly.

Dust-Pressing. The technique of manufacturing clay tiles from *dust-clay*. The damp powdered clay is placed into a screw press and compacted under high pressure to create a tile *body* that is ready for decoration and can be fired without further drying. This method is the basis of all modern mass-produced tiles. (See *Prosser's Patent*)

Earthenware. Clay *bodies* that fire at a comparatively low temperature (700° to 1200°C, 1300° to 2200°F), producing a semi-porous material used for making tiles, bricks, and utilitarian pottery.

Emaux Ombrants. From the French meaning "shadowy enamels." This technique involves *intaglio* molding the surface of a tile or other object and then flooding it with a soft *glaze* that flows freely in the *firing*. The glaze runs off the high points and into the lower recesses of the molding to create a tonal variation. This was the technique used by Sherwin and Cotton and others to create so-called "photographic tiles." These often utilized a dark brown or black glaze to enhance the effect of a photograph.

Enamels. Low temperature colors applied *over-glaze* in a *muffle kiln*. Not as durable as ceramic colors, but available in a much wider variety of shades and effects.

Encaustic Tiles. Tiles with an inlaid pattern created from different colored or stained clays. A die is used to form an *intaglio* pattern in the front of a plastic clay tile and the resulting depressions are filled with a contrasting color of *slip clay*. Encaustic tiles were also produced by *dust-pressing* using a complex system of pierced metal plates or lattices placed in the bottom of the screw press to separate different colored *dust-clays*.

Engobe. A thin layer of slip applied to a tile to provide a surface for decoration (*sgraffito* or *sgraffiato*) or to change the top color of the tile *body*.

Extruded. Tiles that have been formed by squeezing *clay* through a shaped nozzle under high pressure. The process produces a continuous strip, either flat or relief molded, which is then cut into lengths to form the tiles.

Faïence. 1) A *tin-glazed earthenware* painted with a wide palette of *ceramic colors* on a white *tin-glaze* background. Named after the town of Faenza in Italy, a major 15th and 16th century centre for the production of such wares. (See also *Maiolica*.)

Faïence. 2) In the U.K., the term is often applied to large-scale glazed *terra cotta* or frost-proof tiles for architectural use.

Fireclay. A coarse but durable clay that is used for making saggers, the ceramic boxes in which pottery is fired, protecting it from direct contact with the flames. Fireclay is also used to make heavy-duty tiles, some forms of *terra cotta* and *grog*.

Firing. The process of baking ceramics in a *kiln* to create a hard, usable material. (See also: *Biscuit-Firing*; *Glost-Firing*)

Glaze. A thin glass-like film fired onto the surface of ceramics to create a smooth, decorative and protective surface. It can be transparent or opaque, glossy or matt. It seals the surface, making it less prone to dirt and moisture. (See also: *Tin-Glaze*; *Lead-Glaze*; *Over-Glaze*; *Under-Glaze*; *In-Glaze*)

Glaze-Trailing. Applying *glaze* with a broad nozzle (originally a cow-horn or similar), to create a wide line of colored glaze.

Glazing. The process of applying a *glaze*. Glazes can be applied by dipping, brushing, or spraying.

Glost-Firing. The second and/or subsequent *firing* required to fuse the *glaze* to a *biscuit* tile.

Grog. Coarsely ground pre-fired ceramic material, usually fireclay, which is mixed with natural clays to improve workability and strength.

Grout. A cementitious material forced into the joints between tiles after fixing. It keeps moisture and dirt out of the joints and enhances the beauty of the finished product.

Incised. A pattern formed by cutting into the surface of the tile with a sharp point or knife before *firing*.

In-Glaze. A technique of decoration where the pattern is applied to the raw *glaze* before *firing*. During *glost-firing* the design sinks into and becomes an integral part of the *glaze* surface. *Delftware* and *faïence* are typical examples.

Intaglio. A design modeled in sunken relief.

Iznik. A major centre for the production of tiles and pottery in the 16th and 17th centuries. Situated on the site of modern-day Nicaea in Turkey, Iznik wares were famed for the characteristic raised red pigment, known as "Armenian Bole."

Kiln. A large oven for *firing* ceramics. It may be fuelled with coal, wood, oil, electricity, or gas. (See also: *Bottle Kiln*; *Tunnel Kiln*)

Lead-Glaze. A rich, glossy, transparent *glaze* consisting chiefly of various lead compounds. Usually clear, it may be stained with naturally occurring or deliberately added contaminants such as iron oxides (rich brown colors), or copper (shades of green).

Line-Impressed. 1) (medieval) A decorative technique whereby lines are impressed into the surface of the tile which is then glazed.

Line-Impressed. 2) (19th & 20th century) A decorative technique whereby raised lines are molded onto the surface of the tile to resemble *tube-lining*.

Lock-Back. An undercut pattern molded or impressed into the back of a tile during manufacture to prevent the tile working loose from its fixing.

Luster. A vivid iridescence or metallic sheen produced on the surface of ceramics by firing metallic oxides onto the surface of the glaze in a reducing atmosphere. A thin film of pure metal is left on the surface, creating a reflective surface.

Maiolica. A *tin-glazed earthenware* painted with *ceramic colors,* similar to *faïence,* but generally with little if any of the white *tin-glaze* left showing. Probably named after Majorca, a major centre for the export of such wares in the 15th and 16th centuries.

Majolica. *Lead-glazed,* relief molded *earthenware* decorated with opaque, colored *glazes.* Developed by Léon Arnoux for Herbert Minton in 1849 and first exhibited at the Great Exhibition of 1851.

Manganese Purple. A strong purple color produced from manganese ores, used mainly in *faïence, maiolica,* and *delftwares.*

Mosaic. A design created from small pieces (*tesserae*) of ceramic, stone, glass, or other materials.

Muffle Kiln. A special low-temperature *kiln* used for firing enamels and some lusters.

Nail Holes. *Delftware* tiles often have small holes in the front surface, near the corners. These are a result of the use of a wooden template board to cut the tiles to shape before firing. To prevent the board from slipping, small nails are hammered through, leaving the characteristic small holes in two or more corners of the finished tile.

Over-Glaze. Applying decoration to a tile that has already been *glazed,* using *enamels* that are fired at a relatively low temperature in a *muffle kiln.* This is the least durable ceramic decorating technique, as the surface decoration can be rubbed away in time.

Opus Sectile. The technique of shaping tiles to follow the outlines of the design, each tile being a different shape. The technique was originally used with natural stone as a variation of mosaic. In the 1880s, Powells of Whitefriars, London, used the name to describe their own shaped glass tile compositions, and in the early 20th century, the Porcelayne Fles Company of Delft in the Netherlands, used the name Opus Sectiel (sic) to describe their *earthenware* tiles utilizing a similar technique.

Pâte-sur-Pâte. From the French meaning "paste-on-paste." A decorative technique similar to *barbotine* but using thin white *slip* built up painstakingly over a dark colored or stained *body.*

Photographic Tile. Two main techniques have been used to create tiles with a photographic image:

a) The relief molded process; a block of light-sensitive gelatin is exposed through a photographic negative for 24 hours. When the gelatin is washed with water, the areas exposed to the light are washed away leaving a relief image. From this, a mold is created from which the tiles are pressed. A special *glaze* is applied which runs freely in the *firing,* leaving the higher parts of the design showing through. The effect is that of a dark sepia-tone photograph. The term is also applied to relief molded tiles based on photographs and pioneered by George Cartlidge for Sherwin and Cotton.

b) The dusting-on process; a special print is made from the negative using a film that becomes sticky on exposure to light. Ceramic color in powder form is then dusted over the film, where it adheres to the sticky areas. This is then rubbed down onto the tile so that the image is deposited on the surface of the tile. This is then glazed and fired to fix the design.

Plastic Clay. Clay in its natural wet state, or with water added to make it moldable. Plastic clay can be cut to form flat tiles, pressed into a mold to produce relief tiles, or have a pattern impressed into it.

Porcelain. A clay *body* consisting mainly of the natural material kaolin (china clay), fired at a very high temperature (1250° - 1400°C, 2250° to 2550°F). to produce a fine white, impervious material.

Pouncing. A technique of transferring a pattern to a blank tile to aid repetitive design. The outline of the design is drawn on paper (*spons*) and the lines are then pricked through with a pin. Crushed charcoal is then "pounced" through the holes using a small bag (or "pounce") to leave a pattern of dots that guide the painter.

Prosser's Patent. In 1842, Richard Prosser took out a patent for the manufacture of buttons and similar items using *dust clay.* Herbert Minton bought the patent and used it to manufacture *mosaic tesserae* and small tiles. He later developed the technique to make larger tiles up to 12 inches square.

Quarry Tile. 1) In the U.K., quarry tile signifies a fairly coarse, unglazed, plain colored tile used for flooring. These are traditionally made in the same way as bricks, by pressing clay into a wooden mold (slop molding), but in recent times, the term has also been applied to *extruded* tiles.

Quarry Tile. 2) In North America, quarry tile signifies a fine surface plain or decorated floor tile of high quality, usually dust-pressed.

Relief Molded. Tile with a pattern formed in relief from a mold or impressed design. The design can then be *glazed* in a single color or areas can be highlighted in different colored *glazes.*

Rutile Glazes. Glazes made from the ores or refined salts and oxides of uranium, usually producing a vivid orange or red color.

Screen-printing. A piece of taut open-weave silk, metal, or synthetic fabric carries the negative of the desired image in an impervious substance, such as glue; ink is forced through the clear (printing) areas by a squeegee onto the ceramic tile or other material behind.

Sgraffito. A layer of colored *slip* (*engobe*) is applied to the top surface of a tile. The design is then scratched back through the *slip* to the underlying *body* color.

Sgraffiato. Similar to sgraffito, but the *slip* is cut away in broad, flat areas rather than just outlines.

Slip. *Clay* watered down to the consistency of thin cream. This is used to paint (*barbotine*), cover (*engobe*), or otherwise decorate a ceramic surface.

Slip-Trailing. Applying a runny *slip* to the surface of an unfired tile using a broad nozzle. The *slip* spreads out to form a broad outline. This term is sometimes wrongly applied to *tube-lining*.

Spons (plural: **Sponsen**). A pricked paper pattern from which a design is transferred to the tile surface by *pouncing*.

Stencil. A pierced sheet of thin metal, plastic, or paper which is laid over the surface to be decorated, masking off areas to create a pattern by brush-painting or spraying with an *aerograph*.

Stoneware. A *clay body*, naturally rich in silica or with added flint, firing to a high temperature. The resultant body is impervious to moisture and therefore especially suited to external use. Stoneware bodies often incorporate a proportion of *grog* to improve the workability of the clay.

Terra Cotta (U.K.: **Terracotta**). Literally "fired earth"; the term is applied to coarse, unglazed floor tiles (usually red bodied), without decoration. Terra cotta is also used to describe large decorative ceramic blocks used as architectural embellishment, mainly on the exterior of buildings; sometimes structural, sometimes applied as a veneer.

Tessera (plural: **Tesserae**). The small individual pieces of a *mosaic*.

Tin-Glaze. A *lead-glaze* to which a proportion of tin oxide has been added, making the *glaze* white and opaque.

Transfer-printing. Due to irregularities of surface, it is not possible to print directly onto a ceramic surface. In 1756, Sadler and Green of Liverpool developed the technique of printing a design onto thin tissue paper, which was then rubbed face down onto the tile surface, before the ink dried. Initially the inks were made with *enamel* colors applied *over-glaze*, but these were soon superseded by *ceramic colors*, which could be applied *under-glaze*. The earliest Sadler and Green tiles were printed from woodblocks (1756), but within six months, they were using copper plate engravings.

Tube-Lining. A process akin to piping icing onto a cake. *Slip* clay is placed in a squeeze bulb fitted with a fine nozzle. As the bulb is squeezed, a thin line of *clay* is piped onto the surface of the tile, creating raised lines that contain and separate colored *glazes* that are applied after the *slip* has dried.

Tunnel Kiln. Invented in 1914 by Conrad Dressler, a German-born sculptor working in England, the tunnel kiln was the first continuously operating *kiln*. It consists of a long, square tunnel, heated at the middle, through which the tiles are transported on a train of special heatproof wagons, running on rails. Taking up to 24 hours to traverse the tunnel, the tiles gradually rise in temperature and then fall slowly back to cool, thus avoiding thermal shock.

Under-Glaze. The technique of decorating directly onto the *body* of the tile and then applying a transparent or translucent *glaze* over the design. This is the most durable method of ceramic decoration.

Zaffer. Cobalt ore used to produce a rich blue ceramic color.

Where to See Tiles

Museums

U.K.

Victoria & Albert Museum
Cromwell Road
South Kensington
London
SW7 2RL
T: +44 (0) 20 7938 8500

Large collection of Islamic, Italian maiolica, Dutch and English delftware, and 20th century tiles.

The British Museum
Great Russell Street
London
WC1B 3DG
T: +44 (0) 20 7636 1555

Large collection of medieval, Islamic and Victorian tiles.

The Gladstone Pottery Museum
Uttoxeter Road
Longton
Stoke-on-Trent
ST3 1PO
T: +44 (0) 1782 319 232

Large collection of mainly Victorian and 20th century tiles displayed in an old pottery.

The Potteries Museum and Art Gallery
Hanley
Stoke-on-Trent
ST1 4HS
T: +44 (0) 1782 232 323

Large collection of pottery of all kinds including a good selection of tiles.

The Jackfield Tile Museum
(part of the Ironbridge Gorge Museum)
Jackfield
Telford
TF8 7AW
T: +44 (0) 1952 882 030

The former Craven Dunnill & Co. factory now houses an excellent display of 19th and 20th century tiles, mainly from the area around Jackfield. The museum concentrates on the manufacture of tiles and has viewing areas where the production of all types of tile may be seen.

The De Morgan Centre
West Hill Library Building
38 West Hill
London
SW18 1RZ
T: +44 (0) 20 8871 1144

William de Morgan Tiles

France

Musée de la Céramique Architecturale
The Boulenger Museum
432 avenue du Marèchal Foch
60390 Auneuil
T: +33 2 44 47 78 47

Temporarily closed; mainly 19th and early 20th century encaustic tiles.

Maison de la Faïence
rue Jean Macé
62440 Desvres
T: +33 2 21 83 23 23

French 18th and 19th century tin-glazed tiles.

Musée National de Céramique
Place de la Manufacture
92310 Sèvres
T: +33 1 45 34 99 05

French tiles of all periods.

Germany

Erstes Deutsches Fliesenmuseum
Reichenstraße 4
19258 Boizenburg
T: +49 (0) 3 8847 53881

Wonderful collection of German Art Nouveau tiles
(Jugendstilfliesen).

Museum Nienburg
Leinstraße 4
3070 Nienburg
T: +49 (0) 5021 12461

Collection of German and Dutch delftware tiles.

Villeroy & Boch Museum
Postfach 100110
66651 Merzig
T: +49 (0) 6864 812 686

Large collection of Villeroy & Boch tiles and ceramics, including many 20th century examples.

Netherlands

Nederlands Tegelmuseum/Dutch Tile Museum
Eikenzoom 12
6731 BH Otterlo
T: +31 (0) 318 591 519

Dutch delftware and other tiles, including a fascinating collection of Japanese Art Nouveau tiles. Reserve collection, by ap-
pointment only.

Museum Boymans-Van Beuningen
Museumpark 18-20
3015 CX Rotterdam
T: +31 (0) 10 441 9400

Dutch delftware and other tiles.

Museum het Princessehof
Grote Kerkstraat 11
8911 DZ Leeuwarden
T: +31 (0) 58 212 7438

Islamic, North African, Dutch delftware and other tiles

Nederlands Openluchtmuseum
Schelmsweg 89
6816 SJ Arnhem
T: +31 (0) 26 357 6111

Open air museum—reconstructed houses from various parts
of the Netherlands, many of which feature tiles *in-situ*.

Huis Lambert van Meerten
Oude Delft 199
2611 HD Delft
T: +31 (0) 15 260 2358

Dutch delftware tiles.

United States of America

The Cooper-Hewitt Museum
2 East 91st Street
New York, NY 10128
Tel +1 (212) 860 6868

A good representative collection of tiles from around the world.

Philadelphia Museum of Art
26th Street and Benjamin Franklin Parkway
Philadelphia, PA 19101-7646
Tel: +1 (215) 763 8100

A comprehensive collection of delftware tiles.

Taiwan

Taipei County Yingge Ceramics Museum
239 No.200 Wen-Hua Road
Yinko Township
Taipei
R.O.C.
T: +886 2 8677 2727

Representative collections of delftware tiles and Japanese Art
Nouveau tiles.

Tiles in Situ

The Tiles and Architectural Ceramics Society publishes a
comprehensive gazetteer of tile sites accessible to the public
within the United Kingdom (see Bibliography below). The
Society also has an on-line location index pinpointing important tile locations in the U.K. The list is organized by county
and can be found at: www.tilesoc.org.uk.

Websites

The Tiles and Architectural Ceramics Society
www.tilesoc.org.uk

Tiles on the Web
www.tiles.org

The Joy of Shards
www.thejoyofshards.co.uk

Antique Calendar Tiles
www.antiquecalendar.com/tiles

Friends of Terra Cotta
www.preserve.org/fotc

The National Tile Database
www.tessellations.org.uk

The Tile Image Gallery
www.derbycity.com/michael/tile-cd.html

Organizations for Tile Enthusiasts

The Tiles and Architectural Ceramics Society
Membership Secretary
37 Moseley Road
Timperley
Altrincham, Cheshire
WA15 7TF
U.K.
Email: kathbertadams@hotmail.com
Website: www.tilesoc.org

Tile Heritage Foundation
P O Box 1850
Healdsburg, CA 95448
USA
Email: foundation@tileheritage.org
Website: www.tileheritage.org

Friends of Terra Cotta
771 West End Avenue #10E
New York, NY 10025-5572
USA
Email: pstunick@worldnett.att.net
Website: www.preserve.org/fotc

GRECB (Groupe de Recherches et d'Etudes de la Ceramique du Beauvaisis)
8 avenue Victor Hugo
60000 Beauvais
France
(Study group for ceramics and tiles from the Beauvais region)

Stichting Vrienden van het Nederlands Tegelmuseum
p/a Van Tuyllaan 7
5481 RA Schijndel
Netherlands
Email: vrienden.tegelmuseum@tiscali.nl
Website: www.nederlandstegelmuseum.nl
(Friends organization for the Dutch Tile Museum)

Craft and Studio Tile Makers

Nick Abercrombie 1991-

Carne Farm Studio, Nancledra, Penzance, Cornwall

Nick Abercrombie was born in Stafford and has potters in his family, but his first experience of tile making was when working in partnership with Bernard Murphy in South Africa in 1989. Nick found a large Hindu population in South Africa, and discovered that there was a demand for tiles and tile panels depicting Hindu deities to decorate the local temples. On his return to England in 1991, he decided to set up a small studio decorating tiles.

He uses hand painting, silk-screen printing, airbrush, and sponged techniques to create a standard range of designs as well as special commissions. His early work was produced overglaze but after a couple of years he changed to working underglaze on tile blanks bought in from *The Decorative Tile Works* in Jackfield and *H. & E. Smith Ltd*. He also experimented with producing pseudo-encaustic tiles, achieving an inlaid effect on biscuit tile by using colors modified with a high level of flux. Many of the pseudo-encaustic tiles were incorporated into Nick's own pre-cast concrete jardinières.

The tiles are fired in an electric kiln at just over 1000°C. His range of standard tiles includes Neo-Gothic designs, reproductions of old maps and Cornish scenes, as well as his own designs in Art Nouveau style.

Two screen printed tiles, part of a continuous border design based on a Chamberlain encaustic tile of the 1840s. Each tile 6" square. c.1995. H. & E. Smith blanks. Price group A (each).

Hand painted tile with a pseudo delft design, signed on the front "NA '97". 6" square. 1997. Decorative Tile Works blank. Price group A.

Screen printed and hand colored tile with a design taken from an old map of Cornwall. 6" square. c.1995. H. & E. Smith blank. Price group A.

Screen printed and hand colored tile with a mermaid design. 6" square. c.1995. H. & E. Smith blank. Price group A.

Mark Aldridge and Marc Livingstone
Smoke and Fire 1996-

1996-2000: Unit 7A, Meadow View Business Estate, Uffington Road, Stamford, Lincolnshire
2000- : The Granary, Main Road, Darsham, Suffolk

Smoke and Fire was established by friends Mark Aldridge and Marc Livingstone in 1996. Mark had been educated in the Fine Arts and studied ceramics at Dublin College of Art from 1974 to 1976. Marc also had a background in ceramics and when they met in 1996 they formed Smoke and Fire to manufacture tiles. These were initially slip-cast in plaster molds but more recent production has been extruded. They have made a number of different series, including English Garden, Delft, and Atlantic. Mark Aldridge designs and paints most of the tiles himself, although for a short time, some were decorated by Tina Hannay and others. Their Delft tile range is produced on blanks bought in from *Clayworth Potteries* and decorated in-house.

The company has developed its own range of stoneware glaze recipes and fires these in gas and electric kilns to 1250°C, the high temperature imparting a distinctive and varied smoky finish to the glaze.

Screen printed and hand colored tile with a swan design. 6" square. c.1995. H. & E. Smith blank. Price group A.

Identification and Marks
Nick Abercrombie also uses his initials "NJA" or "NA" on the front of some of his hand painted tiles.

Two hand painted plastic clay stoneware tiles with traditional delft designs. 5½" square and 4" square. c.1999. Price group A (each).

Hand painted plastic clay stoneware tile depicting a dragonfly.
5″ square. c.1999. Price group A.

Hand painted plastic clay
stoneware tile depicting an apple. 5″
square. c.1999. Price group A.

Hand painted plastic clay stoneware tile depicting a tulip. 5″ square.
c.1999. Price group A.

Hand painted plastic clay stoneware tile depicting a sailing barge from the
"Maritime" range. 5″ square. c.1999. Price group A.

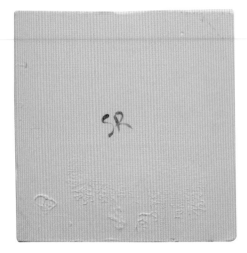

Hand painted plastic clay stoneware tile depicting a seashell. 5" square. c.1999. Price group A.

Plastic clay wall tile. 5" square. 1996- . Most Smoke and Fire tiles are unmarked, but occasional examples have the artist's initials painted as shown here.

Charles Allen
(Newcastle Arts Centre) 1983-1991
New Castle Delft 1991-

1983-1991: Newcastle Arts Centre, Newcastle upon Tyne
1991-1993: Albion Row, Newcastle upon Tyne
1993- : 25B Hoults Estate, Walker Road, Newcastle upon Tyne

Charles Allen has been making tiles since 1983, when he worked for a trading division of Newcastle Arts Centre that produced handmade tiles for floors, mainly encaustic. He established his own company, New Castle Delft, in 1991 and in 1993 he took over historic premises in what was formerly the Maling Ford B Pottery. In its day, the Maling Pottery was one of the largest potteries in the world, established in 1762 in Sunderland. The Maling Ford B works was built in 1878 and closed in 1963, when it was turned into a number of craft workshops. In his new business, Charles decided upon a change of direction to focus on wall tiles, allowing him to explore and exploit a broader range of decorative techniques. His earliest tiles were traditional delft in style, both polychrome and classic blue and white, but his repertoire has expanded to include handmade, hand painted, molded, encaustic, tube-lined, glaze painted, and transfer printed tiles. He has even ventured into the field of salt glaze stoneware, producing edging tiles for a garden restoration project in the north east of England. The stoneware clay for these tiles was quarried and milled in Northumberland and they were fired in one of the Maling Pottery's original coal-burning kilns dating from the 1930s. Although most tiles are made to commission, some designs that have been featured on the company's website have been repeated many times over.

Since graduating with an Arts degree in 1982, Charles has been involved with community arts projects throughout his local area. The majority of these projects have been school-based placements and residencies, where he has worked with students and staff to create site-specific artworks. These have mainly consisted of ceramic murals and panels but have also included painted murals, stone carving, and plaster work. Charles has also been involved in a number of restoration projects, particularly during 1996-97, when he worked on the restoration of the faïence frontage of the Beehive Hotel, a listed building in the Bigg Market area of Newcastle, as well as the former Shakespeare Public House in Middlesbrough.

Charles forms his tiles in wooden molds from plastic clays; earthenware and stoneware, in buff, white and terra cotta. Sawdust is used as a release in the wooden mold and this burns out in the kiln, leaving a distinctive rough finish to the backs of the tiles. The tiles are generally given a white or ivory tin-glaze or a clear glaze. For the designs, he uses oxides, under-glaze colors, over-glaze colors, and occasionally lusters. Firing takes place in an electric kiln. He has also on occasion decorated commercial blanks from *H. & R. Johnson Ltd.* and others.

Panel of six hand painted tiles depicting "Houseboats," designed and painted by Charles Allen. Each tile 6" square. 1990s. *Courtesy of and photograph by Charles Allen.* Price group C (panel).

Set of four hand painted tiles depicting "The Angel of the North," designed and painted by Charles Allen. Each tile 6" square. c.2000. *Courtesy of and photograph by Charles Allen.* Price group A (each).

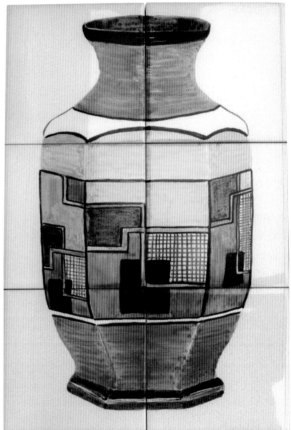

Panel of nine hand painted tiles depicting "Clarice Cliffe" and some of the designs she created during the 1920s and 1930s, designed and painted by Charles Allen. Each tile 6" square. 1990s. *Courtesy of and photograph by Charles Allen.* Price group D (panel).

Panel of six hand painted tiles depicting a Clarice Cliffe vase, designed and painted by Charles Allen. Each tile 6" square. 1990s. H. & R. Johnson blanks. *Courtesy of and photograph by Charles Allen.* Price group C (panel).

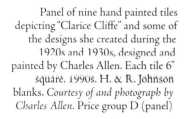

Panel of nine hand painted tiles depicting "Clarice Cliffe" and some of the designs she created during the 1920s and 1930s, designed and painted by Charles Allen. Each tile 6" square. 1990s. H. & R. Johnson blanks. *Courtesy of and photograph by Charles Allen.* Price group D (panel)

Panel of nine hand painted plastic clay tiles depicting fish, designed and painted by Charles Allen. Each tile 4" square. 1990s. *Courtesy of and photograph by Charles Allen.* Price group D (panel)

Set of fifteen hand painted plastic clay tiles depicting stylized houses, designed and painted by Charles Allen. Each tile 4" square. 1990s. *Courtesy of and photograph by Charles Allen.* Price group A (each).

Set of six hand painted plastic clay tiles depicting stylized landscapes and cityscapes, designed and painted by Charles Allen. Each tile 4" square. 1990s. *Courtesy of and photograph by Charles Allen.* Price group A (each).

Hand painted and crackle glaze plastic clay tile depicting bridges, designed and painted by Charles Allen. 6" square. 1990s. *Courtesy of and photograph by Charles Allen.* Price group A.

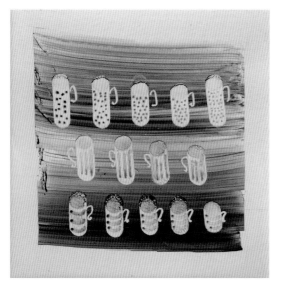

Hand painted and sgraffito tile depicting mugs, designed and painted by Charles Allen. 150mm square. 1997. Argentine commercial blank. *Courtesy of Maggie Angus Berkowitz*. Price group A.

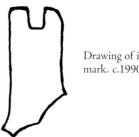

Drawing of impressed mark. c.1990-c.1999

Drawing of impressed mark. c.1990-c.1999.

Identification and Marks

Drawing of impressed mark. c.1990-c.1999.

Drawing of impressed mark. c.1983-c.1990.

Painted mark. 1996- . The centre "S" is enlarged in commemoration of the 1996 death of Charlie's father, with whom he shares the Christian name, Stanley.

Drawing of impressed mark. c.1983-c.1990.

www.newcastledelft.com

Drawing of impressed mark. c.1999-2005.

Molly Attrill 1986-

The Pottery, Mersley Farm, Newchurch, Isle of Wight

Molly Attrill's introduction to clay and pottery came when she studied with Michael Leach at Yelland Manor Pottery, North Devon, in 1973. After further studies at the West Surrey College of Art and Design from 1974-1977, she worked in a number of studios in Canada and France and finally established her own pottery on the Isle of Wight in 1982.

Since 1986, she has made small numbers of hand-cut earthenware tiles in tin-glaze with oxide-painted decoration. These are fired in a neutral atmosphere in an LPG (Liquefied Petroleum Gas) fired kiln. Most of her work, both individual tiles and panels, is usually made to commission. She has undertaken a number of commercial commissions on the Isle of Wight, including panels for the café and kitchen of St. Mary's Hospital, Newport and a large panel for the Quay Arts Centre, also in Newport. She has also experimented with inlaid tiles.

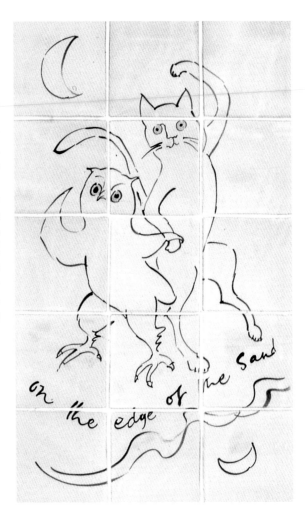

Panel of fifteen hand painted plastic clay tiles depicting "on the edge of the sand" from the poem "The Owl and the Pussycat." Each tile 4" square. 1999. *Courtesy of Molly Attrill*. Price group D (panel).

Panel of fifteen hand painted plastic clay tiles depicting "a year and a day" from the poem "The Owl and the Pussycat." Each tile 4" square. 1999. *Courtesy of Molly Attrill*. Price group D (panel).

Plastic clay encaustic tile depicting a greyhound. 6" square. 1999. *Courtesy of Molly Attrill*. Price group A.

Panel of sixteen hand painted plastic clay tiles depicting "Sicilian Buttercup." Each tile 4" square. 1999. *Courtesy of Molly Attrill.* Price group D (panel).

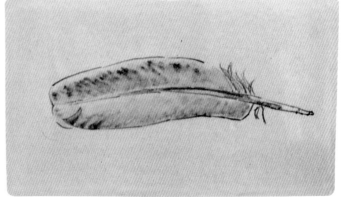

Two hand painted plastic clay tiles depicting feathers. Each tile 4" x 8". 1999. *Courtesy of Molly Attrill.* Price group A.

Identification and Marks

Panel of sixteen hand painted plastic clay tiles depicting "La Fleche." Each tile 4" square. 1999. *Courtesy of Molly Attrill* Price group D (panel).

Impressed mark. 1986-

Diana Barraclough
Diana Barraclough Ceramics 1966-

25 The Croft, Hungerford, Berkshire

Diana Barraclough gained her degree in ceramics at Bournemouth & Poole College of Art and has run her own pottery since 1973, although her interest in tiles started back in 1966. She specializes in hand-rolled tiles with applied clay relief impressed with tools etc. She also uses slip-trailing and sgraffito techniques and fires her tiles at a reduced stoneware temperature. She says, "Although I'm a potter I have always made tiles. For me they are paintings in clay. The sea and birds are my main subjects." During the 1980s, she undertook a number of large tile panels but has since reverted to making individual one-off tiles.

Composite hand sculpted tile consisting of sixteen small fish and wave tiles set on a stoneware base tile. Each small tile 2" square, base tile 11" square. c.2000. *Courtesy of and photograph by Diana Barraclough.* Price group B.

Hand sculpted tile in stoneware on white scarva clay body depicting a Cornish coastal scene. 6" square. c.2000. *Courtesy of and photograph by Diana Barraclough.* Price group A.

Hand sculpted tile in stoneware on white scarva clay body depicting a seascape. 6" square. c.2000. *Courtesy of and photograph by Diana Barraclough.* Price group A.

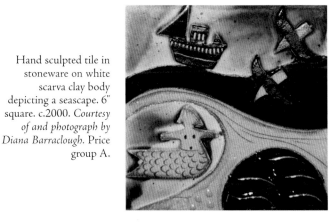

Hand sculpted tile in stoneware depicting a beach scene. 7" square. 1997. *Courtesy of and photograph by Diana Barraclough.* Price group A.

Impressed mark used 1966-1980.

Impressed mark used after 1980.

Hand sculpted tile in stoneware depicting a cormorant. 10" square. c.2000. *Courtesy of and photograph by Diana Barraclough.* Price group B.

John M. Bass (1920-2005)
Mynde Ceramics c.1968-2002

c.1968-1972: West Kilbride, Scotland
1972-1984: Main Street, West Kilbride, Scotland
1984-1994: Own Studio, Ardrossan, Scotland
1994-2002: Studio 'K/L' The Courtyard Studios, Harbourside, Irvine, Scotland

John Bass started tile decorating as a hobby in the late 1960s. He was self-taught and began with two small electric kilns in the basement of his home in West Kilbride. He later moved into premises in Main Street, West Kilbride, fronted by a shop, where he undertook commissions for private clients—usually bathrooms, kitchens, halls in private houses, and bars in restaurants (including a hotel bar in Portpatrick). He produced screen printed and hand painted tiles, mainly on *H. & R. Johnson* blanks, and also carried a large stock of transfer prints. He occasionally made his own relief molded tiles.

The opening nearby of a large branch of a national do-it-yourself company was an overnight disaster for the business, so John moved to a studio in Ardrossan and diversified into wall plaques, coasters, clocks and mirrors, house names and numbers, etc. These were sold through local craft fairs and shops all over Scotland and into England, as well as to museums in Glasgow, where his Charles Rennie Mackintosh-inspired tiles were very popular. The Mackintosh Exhibition held at the McLellan Galleries in 1996 added to their success.

John was widowed in the early 1990s and immersed himself in his work, moving to new studios in Irvine in 1994. He began to experiment with different design techniques, including a pottery wheel, different glazes, glass fusion, and the use of a blowtorch. The Design Centre in London displayed some of his experimental work, but sadly it didn't sell.

At age seventy-five, John met and married his second wife, Ina-Mae, who helped him in the pottery until his reluctant retirement in 2002 due to failing eyesight and frailty. He tried unsuccessfully to sell the business for two years, but sadly there was no one willing to take it on and the studio finally closed in April 2002. John died in January 2005, aged eighty-four.

Hand sculpted tile in stoneware depicting birds and fish. 8" square. c.2000. *Courtesy of and photograph by Diana Barraclough.* Price group B.

The Tawny Owl

Screen printed tile depicting "The Tawny Owl," one of a series based on the woodcuts of Thomas Bewick. 6" square. 1979. H. & R. Johnson blank. Price group A.

Screen printed trade tile featuring a design based on the work of Charles Rennie Mackintosh. 2" x 4¼". c.1995. H. & R. Johnson blank. Price group B.

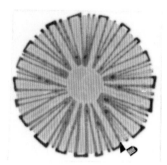 

Two experimental screen printed and hand decorated tiles with abstract designs by John M. Bass. Each tile 6" square. c.1995. H. & R. Johnson blanks. *Courtesy of and photograph by Ina-Mae Bass.* Price group B (each tile).

Transfer printed tile depicting a female figure in Art Nouveau style, based on an early 20th century design by Jessie M. King; made as an advertising tile for "Miss Cranston's Lunch and Tea Rooms" in Glasgow. 6" x 3". c.1995. H. & R. Johnson blank. Price group B.

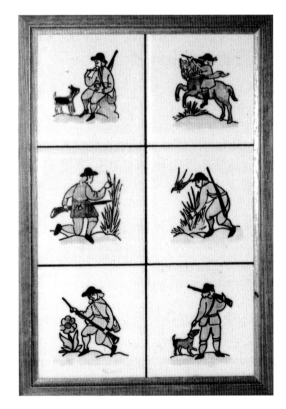

Set of six transfer printed tiles depicting hunting scenes, designed by John M. Bass. Each tile 6" square. c.1995. H. & R. Johnson blanks. *Courtesy of and photograph by Ina-Mae Bass.* Price Group A (each tile).

Left: transfer printed tile depicting a fish designed by John M. Bass. Right: screen printed and glaze colored tile depicting a duck designed by John M. Bass. Left tile: 100mm x 200mm, right tile: 100mm square. Unknown commercial blanks. *Courtesy of and photograph by Ina-Mae Bass.* Price group A (each tile).

Geoff Beeston
Badger Pottery 1962-

1962-1968: Kenya
1968-1973: 20 Cardigan Street, Oxford
1973- : 125B Main Road, Long Hanborough, Witney, Oxfordshire

The first tiles Geoff Beeston painted depicted a seahorse and a tropical fish for two friends who were getting married. This was while he was a student in 1959. He continued to paint a few tiles until he moved to Kenya in 1962, where he went to dive. The tropical fish and other animals he saw inspired him to paint more tiles. When he returned to England in 1968, he started the Badger Pottery as a commercial venture, making earthenwares and painting tiles. He was also inspired by British wildlife and created a range of very atmospheric designs depicting mammals by moonlight, many of which have been in production for over thirty years.

Identification and Marks

Self adhesive label on cork back (H. & R. Johnson blank). 6" square tile. c.1972-c.1984.

JOHN M BASS
STUDIO 'K/L'
The Courtyard Studios
HARBOURSIDE
IRVINE, SCOTLAND
KA12 8PZ
01294 271127

Self adhesive label on H. & R. Johnson blank. 2" x 4¼" tile. 1994-2002.

Hand painted and sgraffito tile depicting a "Red Deer Hind," titled and signed on back "Geoff Beeston, Badger Pottery, Oxford." 6" square. 1971. H. & R. Johnson blank. *Courtesy of Thelma Shepley.* Price group B.

Geoff works mainly with pre-glazed tiles, which were initially bought in from *H. & R. Johnson Ltd.* and occasionally *Hereford Tiles Ltd.* He uses sable brushes to apply under-glaze colors, occasionally with some extra glaze, before firing in an electric kiln at between 1060°C and 1080°C. In more recent years, Geoff has been using *Pilkington's Tiles Ltd.* blanks and commercial tiles bought in from Brazil. He would still prefer to use the old H. & R. Johnson Ltd. twice fired tiles, as these gave softer results with the beautiful brown glazes that he loves to use, but these are no longer available. On his earlier tiles, he often used a sgraffito technique but his more recent tiles rely purely on brushwork. Geoff has also experimented with trailed work and what he refers to as "graffiti." During the 1970s, he also made a small number of tile panels in the form of a crossword puzzle.

Hand painted, stenciled, and sgraffito tile depicting a hare in moonlight. 6" square. 1973. H. & R. Johnson blank. *Courtesy of Roger Hensman*. Price group A.

Stenciled and sgraffito tile depicting a bear. 6" diameter. 1972. H. & R. Johnson blank. *Courtesy of Mary Bentley*. Price group A.

Stenciled and sgraffito tile depicting a hedgehog in moonlight. 6" square. 1973. H. & R. Johnson blank. *Courtesy of Roger Hensman*. Price group A.

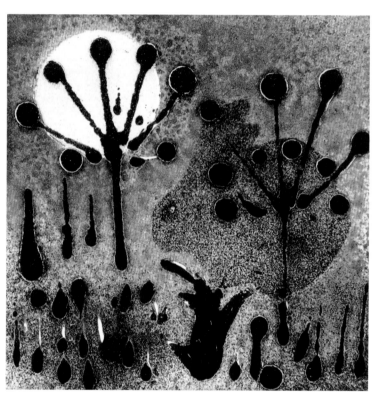

Stenciled and sgraffito tile depicting an owl in moonlight. 6" square. 1973. H. & R. Johnson blank. Price group A.

Hand painted, stenciled, and sgraffito tile depicting a rabbit in moonlight. 6" square. 1973. H. & R. Johnson blank. *Courtesy of Roger Hensman.* Price group A.

Hand painted, stenciled, and sgraffito tile depicting a fox in moonlight. 6" square. 1973. H. & R. Johnson blank. *Courtesy of Thelma Shepley.* Price group A.

Hand painted, stenciled, and sgraffito tile depicting a deer in moonlight. 6"
square. 1974. H. & R. Johnson blank. Price group A.

Stenciled tile depicting a badger. 6" square. 1975. H. & R. Johnson blank.
Price group A.

Hand painted, stenciled, and sgraffito tile depicting an otter. 6" diameter.
1975. H. & R. Johnson blank. Price group A.

Hand painted, stenciled, and sgraffito tile depicting a deer. 6" square in contemporary frame. 1978. H. & R. Johnson blank. *Courtesy of Mary Bentley.* Price group A.

Stenciled tile depicting a hedgehog. 6" diameter. 1980. H. & R. Johnson blank. Price group A.

Cheese board incorporating two stenciled tiles depicting pigs. Each tile 6" square. c.1985. H. & R. Johnson blanks. Price group B.

Stenciled and sgraffito tile depicting a fox. 6" square. 1978. H. & R. Johnson blank. Price group A.

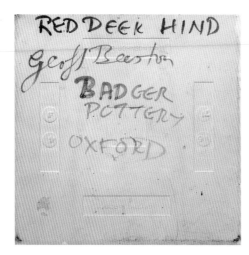

Hand painted mark on H. & R. Johnson 6" square blank. Early 1970s. This tile 1971. *Courtesy of Thelma Shepley.*

Rubber stamp mark on H. & R. Johnson 6" square blank. Late 1970s. This tile 1978.

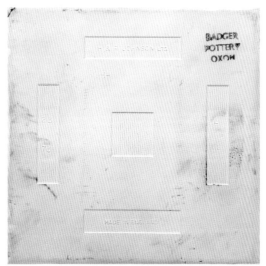

Rubber stamp mark on H. & R. Johnson 6" square blank. Early 1970s. This tile 1973. *Courtesy of Thelma Shepley.*

Quentin Bell (1910-1996)

1936-1969: Charleston, Firle, Sussex
1969-1996: Fulham Pottery

Quentin Bell was born in 1910, the middle son of Clive and Vanessa Bell, and from the age of six he lived at Charleston Farmhouse in East Sussex with his mother and Duncan Grant. Duncan and Vanessa had been co-directors of the Omega Workshops (1913-1919), where they had produced hand decorated fabrics and pottery. When they moved to Charleston in 1916, they continued their artistic pursuits and Quentin Bell grew up surrounded by their paintings, fabrics, and pots.

Sgraffito stoneware tile with a female portrait. 4" square. c.1970. *Courtesy of Thelma Shepley.* Price group C.

In 1936, he went to Stoke-on-Trent to learn about pottery from Thomas Fennemore, a director of Brain & Co., a commercial pottery. Quentin used the family pottery at Charleston until he built a larger new pottery in 1939, although he seldom used this until after the Second World War. His first pots were made from the local blue clay, but at high temperatures this formed triple silicate of iron and collapsed like glass in the kiln. He then used red clay from nearby Uckfield in Sussex until supplies ran out in the 1940s.

Quentin continued potting at Charleston until 1969, when he moved to London and began to work with the Fulham Pottery where he produced a small range of handmade tiles with hand painted and sgraffito decoration in tin-glaze.

Identification and Marks

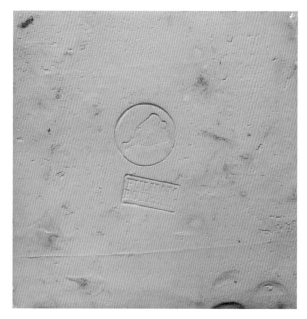

Plastic clay wall tile with impressed Fulham Pottery and Quentin Bell marks. 4" square. 1970s. *Courtesy of Thelma Shepley.*

Sgraffito stoneware tile depicting "Ariadne." 4" square. c.1975. *Courtesy of Roger Hensman.* Price group C.

Sgraffito stoneware tile with a female portrait. 4" square. c.1978. *Courtesy of Thelma Shepley.* Price group C.

Plastic clay wall tile with elaborate impressed Fulham Pottery/Quentin Bell mark. 4" square. 1970s. *Courtesy of Thelma Shepley.*

Plastic clay wall tile with elaborate impressed Fulham Pottery/Quentin Bell mark (twice). 4" square. 1970s. *Courtesy of Roger Hensman.*

References

Anscombe, Isabelle. *Omega and After, Bloomsbury and the Decorative Arts.* London: Thames & Hudson, 1981.

Nicholson, Virginia. *Charleston, An Artists' Home.* Firle, Sussex: The Charleston Trust, 1999.

Maggie Angus Berkowitz
Maggie Angus Berkowitz Tiles 1970-

21/23 Park Road, Milnthorpe, Cumbria

From her workshop in Cumbria, Maggie Berkowitz produces ceramic murals and painted tiles of great verve and humor, both for specific commissions and also for her own enjoyment. Maggie's involvement with making and decorating ceramics grew from her love and knowledge of pottery, which resulted from a three-month temporary placement at Ambleside Pottery. Further theoretical knowledge and practical skills were refined at the Central School of Art, before she took up a teaching post in Cambridge, where she taught teachers at the Cambridge Institute of Education. When she was made homeless and lost her workshop, Maggie applied for a scholarship to go to Italy, eventually finding a placement at the Tre Felci Tile Factory, a small family-run workshop between Salerno and Amalfi. In Italy, she found that although there was

an active government sponsorship that allowed ceramic creativity to flourish, this went hand-in-hand with a cavalier attitude towards the worker. During her year (1959) at the Istituto Statale d'Arte per la Ceramica in Faenza, Maggie reveled in the day-to-day companionship of ceramic students from across the globe, each encouraged to develop specialized skills in what was still a craft based industry. She was also given the task of listing all the silicates used in the school, something that would stand her in good stead in later life.

Following marriage, Maggie moved to New York with her family, returning to the U.K. with her four children some years later. She moved to Cumbria in 1970 to take up a teaching post, and began to establish her reputation as a ceramic artist. She experimented with tube-lining and slip-trailing, and her knowledge of natural science led her to mix and experiment with glazes. Her first commission, for a series of bathroom tiles, came from a family friend. She started making multi-tile panels, but sales were few and far between. Maggie's big break came when she was offered an exhibition at Abbott Hall. Here she not only sold a few panels but also started to make contact with architects and designers around the Lake District. Other exhibitions followed, at which she sold enough work to enable her to buy the materials to continue with her art. Summer holidays, when her children would travel to the U.S.A. to stay with their father, offered Maggie the opportunity to concentrate on her craft, especially as she had agreed with the school that she could use their facilities during the vacation.

It was not until after Maggie had taken early retirement in the mid 1980s that she won her first big commercial commission—a large mural for Langdale Estate, the first Lake District time-share development. Commissions continued in a sporadic fashion, and she was admitted into the Craftsmen Potters Association, one of very few ceramic tile artists in the C.P.A. at the time. By this time, Maggie had a growing reputation and more commissions followed. One of the most prominent was the Appleby War Memorial Swimming Pool, commissioned by Eden Arts in partnership with a range of other arts bodies. The design stemmed from her research into the history of Appleby, and from talking to local residents. It is headed by the town's skyline and depicts the pleasures of swimming against a background that echoes the stone arches of the town's cloisters. Local themes and characters are depicted within each arch. The work illustrates the wide variety of techniques Maggie brings to her work. Her images are drawn directly onto each tile and built up in a number of glaze applications, using techniques that include brushing, pouring, spraying, tube-lining, and wax resist. The tiles are fired after each application of glaze; this repetition results in a luxurious texture and depth of color. The Appleby panel was mounted in an extruded frame produced by fellow Cumbrian ceramicist *Paul Scott.* At the bottom are the words "Look around you and remember"; a phrase suggested by Wren's dedication at St Paul's Cathedral.

Not all Maggie's commissions have been for internal locations. At Low Furness Church of England Primary School, Great Urswick, Cumbria, Maggie devised a 30 meter circular paved area with a central glazed panel depicting the City of Jerusalem. The surrounding pavers were configured as a labyrinth to involve the children in constructive play. She continues to work with great vigor, and her output is most varied, from figurative Aga backs to a giant snakes and ladders board realized on quarry tiles. She has produced signage for public toilets at Carnforth in Lancashire, landscapes and still life panels for the staff dining room at Newton Green Hospital Leeds in Yorkshire, a sundial for Harlow Carr Gardens, Harrogate in Yorkshire, and a plinth for the Hiroshima Peace Park in Japan. Maggie has a close affinity with Japan and has visited that country a number of times in recent years. Her trips have included working visits to the town that gave its name to pottery in Japan, "Seto mono," and to the large commercial factories of INAX, Japan's largest commercial tile manufacturer for whom she works as a freelance designer.

Maggie continues to produce her own work on a domestic scale, from family portraits for a sunroom floor to a jungle themed bathroom. She has also produced a series of tiles entitled "How to wear a cat," which captures her gifts as a figurative artist and the sense of humor that suffuses her work. The dedication that has carried Maggie Berkowitz through the many twists and setbacks of her long career is still much in evidence. She continues to campaign for a "percentage for art" and passionately believes in the importance of art to society, something that was brought home to her during her time in Africa. She is now established as a major ceramic artist and an enduring inspiration for the current generation of craftsmen designers working in tile.

Maggie has used a variety of tile blanks over the years, including wall tiles from *H. & R. Johnson Ltd.* and *Pilkington's Tiles Ltd.*, and floor tiles from Daniel Platt & Son and *George Woolliscroft & Son.*

Slip trailed and hand painted tile, "Madonna." 6" square. 1980s. George Woolliscroft & Son black body floor tile blank. *Courtesy of Maggie Angus Berkowitz.* Price group B.

Panel of nine hand painted tiles with a portrait of Maggie Berkowitz's daughter aged fourteen. Each tile 6" square in original frame. 1970s. Unknown commercial blanks. *Courtesy of Maggie Angus Berkowitz.* Price group E (panel).

Glaze trailed and hand painted tile (low flux glazes), "Lady of the Evening Faces." 200mm square in original frame. 1990s. INAX (Japan) blank. This tile was decorated during one of Maggie Berkowitz's many visits to Japan. *Courtesy of Maggie Angus Berkowitz.* Price group C.

Panel of four hand painted and glaze trailed tiles, "Swimming Thro' the Daisies." Each tile 6" square. 1990s. Pilkington's Tiles blanks. *Courtesy of Maggie Angus Berkowitz.* Price group D (panel).

Glaze trailed and hand painted tile (low flux glazes), "Bamboo." 600mm x 300mm in original frame. 1990s. INAX (Japan) blank. This tile was decorated during one of Maggie Berkowitz's many visits to Japan. *Courtesy of Maggie Angus Berkowitz.* Price group C.

Panel of four hand painted and glaze trailed tiles from the "How to Wear a Cat" series. Each tile 6" square. 1990s. H. & R. Johnson blanks. *Courtesy of Maggie Angus Berkowitz.* Price group D (panel).

Hand painted and glaze trailed tile from the "Member of the Wedding" series. 6" square. 1990s. H. & R. Johnson blank. *Courtesy of Maggie Angus Berkowitz.* Price group C.

Panel of four hand painted and glaze trailed tiles from the "How to Wear a Cat" series. Each tile 6" square. 1990s Pilkington's Tiles blanks. *Courtesy of Maggie Angus Berkowitz.* Price group D (panel).

Hand painted tile from the "Member of the Wedding" series. 6" square. 1990s. Dennis Ruabon quarry tile blank. *Courtesy of Maggie Angus Berkowitz.* Price group C.

Panel of eight hand painted and slip trailed tiles, "The Wren Mermaid." Each tile 6" square. 1990s. Unknown quarry tile blanks. This panel was a prototype for a panel made for Wren House, London, the headquarters of the Women's Royal Naval Reserve. *Courtesy of Maggie Angus Berkowitz*. Price group F (panel)

Panel of four hand painted tiles depicting a woodland scene from Milnthorpe in the Lake District. Each tile 6" square. 1990s. Pilkington's Tiles blanks. *Courtesy of Maggie Angus Berkowitz*. Price group D (panel).

Glaze trailed tile depicting a bird. 6" square. 1990s. Pilkington's Tiles blank. *Courtesy of Maggie Angus Berkowitz*. Price group B.

Experimental tile depicting a girl's head. 6" square. 1990s. Pilkington's Tiles blank. *Courtesy of Maggie Angus Berkowitz*. Price group B.

Hand painted tile depicting a flower. 6" square in original frame. 1990s. Pilkington's Tiles blank. *Courtesy of Maggie Angus Berkowitz*. Price group B.

Hand painted and glaze trailed tile depicting a bird. 6" square in original frame. 1990s. Pilkington's Tiles blank. *Courtesy of Maggie Angus Berkowitz*. Price group B.

Hand painted and glaze trailed tile, "Muffler," from the "Cat" series. 12" square. 1990s. Pilkington's Tiles porcelain blank. *Courtesy of Maggie Angus Berkowitz*. Price group D.

Hand painted and glaze trailed tile depicting a girl's head. 6" square. 1990s. Dennis Ruabon quarry tile blank. *Courtesy of Maggie Angus Berkowitz.* Price group B.

Panel of four hand painted and glaze trailed tiles with a portrait of "Grandchild and Dog." Each tile 6" square. 1990s. Pilkington's Tiles blanks. *Courtesy of Maggie Angus Berkowitz.* Price group D (panel).

Hand painted and glaze trailed tile depicting a bird. 6" square. 1990s. Dennis Ruabon quarry tile blank. *Courtesy of Maggie Angus Berkowitz.* Price group B.

Briglin Pottery 1948-1990 (Tiles 1970s)

Crawford Street, London W1

The Briglin Pottery was established in 1948 by Brigitte Goldschmidt and Eileen Lewenstein to produce well-designed, attractive pottery that could be used in the home and sold at affordable prices. The ladies had met at the pottery belonging to Donald Mills and for the first four years of their venture he worked with them at the Briglin Pottery. They specialized in white glazed earthenwares with painted decoration produced in a distinctive style that was quite unique at the time but was well received and sold successfully. In 1950, Brigitte married and became Brigitte Appleby. Eileen left the firm in 1959 to set up her own studio.

During the 1970s, the company produced a number of tiles painted in dark oxides over a red floor tile body, usually supplied by *Pilkington's & Carter Ltd*. The tiles were fired to stoneware temperature, giving a distinctive matt finish.

Panel of four hand painted and glaze trailed tiles, "Red Tulips." Each tile 6" square. 1990s. Pilkington's Tiles blanks. *Courtesy of Maggie Angus Berkowitz*. Price group D (panel).

Maggie Angus Berkowitz in her studio in Milnthorpe.

Hand painted tile with a floral design. 6" square in original frame. c.1974. Pilkington's + Carter blank. *Courtesy of Adrian Grater*. Price group B.

Identification and Marks

Maggie Berkowitz used this painted mark until she discovered that it meant "down with" in Italian. More recent tiles are sometimes marked with her signature in full.

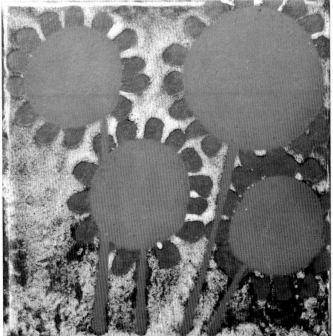

Hand painted tile with an abstract design. 6" square in original frame. c.1974. Pilkington's + Carter blank. *Courtesy of Adrian Grater.* Price group B.

Hand painted tile with an abstract floral design. 6" square. 1976. Pilkington's + Carter blank. *Courtesy of Adrian Grater.* Price group B.

Identification and Marks

No identifying marks.

References

Arnold, Anthea. *Briglin Pottery, 1948-1990.* London: Briglin Books, 2002.

Carlo Briscoe & Edward Dunn
Reptile 1988-

1988-1994: 494 Archway Road, London N6
1994- : Gwaith Menyn, Llanglydwen, Whitland, Dyfed

Edward Dunn and Carlo Briscoe established Reptile in 1988 to create hand painted tiles in the traditional maiolica technique. Their inspiration is drawn mainly from the sea and things nautical. They produce a wide range of standard designs, all hand painted, in a number of different series. They also work to commission and have undertaken a number of large-scale installations for Waitrose Supermarkets, including special panels in the Kings Road, Chelsea, and Marylebone High Street, London branches.

Their tiles are hand painted using oxides and stains on tin-glaze, applied to mainly *H. & R. Johnson Ltd.* biscuit, although sometimes they manufacture their own handmade blanks. Firing is done in an electric kiln at 1040°C.

Series Tiles:

Series Name	Designer	Number of Designs
Sea Life Tiles	Edward Dunn & Carlo Briscoe	30
Nautical Tiles	Edward Dunn & Carlo Briscoe	20 + additional border designs
Flower Tiles	Edward Dunn & Carlo Briscoe	15 + 3 matching border designs
Seabirds	Edward Dunn & Carlo Briscoe	16
Lighthouses	Edward Dunn & Carlo Briscoe	16
Poultry	Edward Dunn & Carlo Briscoe	16
Encircled Birds	Edward Dunn & Carlo Briscoe	16
Encircled Flowers	Edward Dunn & Carlo Briscoe	16

Hand painted tile with a flower design by Edward Dunn and Carlo Briscoe. 6" square. c.1999. H. & R. Johnson blank. *Courtesy of Edward Dunn and Carlo Briscoe.* Price group A.

Hand painted tile with a flower design by Edward Dunn and Carlo Briscoe. 6" square. c.1999. H. & R. Johnson blank. *Courtesy of Edward Dunn and Carlo Briscoe.* Price group A.

Hand painted tile depicting a tug boat, designed by Edward Dunn and Carlo Briscoe. 6" square. c.1999. H. & R. Johnson blank. *Courtesy of Edward Dunn and Carlo Briscoe.* Price group A.

Hand painted tile depicting a tug boat, designed by Edward Dunn and Carlo Briscoe. 6" square. c.1999. H. & R. Johnson blank. *Courtesy of Edward Dunn and Carlo Briscoe.* Price group A.

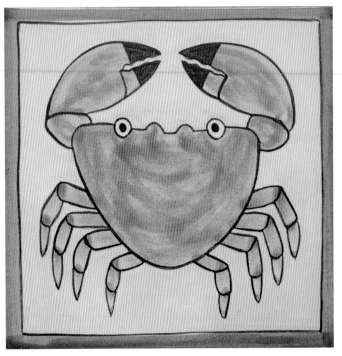

Hand painted tile with a crab design by Edward Dunn and Carlo Briscoe. 6" square. c.1999. H. & R. Johnson blank. *Courtesy of Edward Dunn and Carlo Briscoe*. Price group A.

Hand painted tile with a fish design by Edward Dunn and Carlo Briscoe. 6" square. c.1999. H. & R. Johnson blank. *Courtesy of Edward Dunn and Carlo Briscoe*. Price group A.

Two hand painted tiles with bird and flower designs by Edward Dunn and Carlo Briscoe. Each tile 100mm square. c.1999. H. & R. Johnson blank. *Courtesy of Edward Dunn and Carlo Briscoe*. Price group A (each).

Two hand painted tiles with hen designs by Edward Dunn and Carlo Briscoe. Each tile 100mm square. c.1999. H. & R. Johnson blank. *Courtesy of Edward Dunn and Carlo Briscoe.* Price group A (each).

Two hand painted tiles depicting a cormorant and a seagull, designed by Edward Dunn and Carlo Briscoe. Each tile 100mm square. c.1999. H. & R. Johnson blank. *Courtesy of Edward Dunn and Carlo Briscoe.* Price group A (each).

Two hand painted tiles depicting lighthouses, designed by Edward Dunn and Carlo Briscoe. Each tile 100mm square. c.1999. H. & R. Johnson blank. *Courtesy of Edward Dunn and Carlo Briscoe.* Price group A (each).

Identification and Marks

Rubber stamp mark on H. & R. Johnson 6" square blank. 1990s.

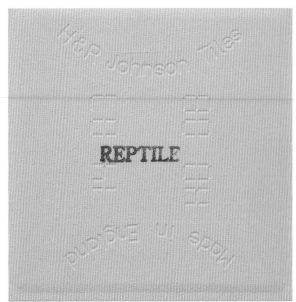

Rubber stamp mark on H. & R. Johnson 4¼" square blank. 1990s.

John Burgess
John Burgess Tiles 1983-1995

Unit B25, Maws Craft Center, Ironbridge Gorge Museum, Jackfield, Telford, Shropshire

John "Bud" Burgess was one of the first craftsmen to take space in the newly refurbished Maws Craft Centre created in the early 1980s from part of the original Victorian Maws Tile factory. He acquired an old flywheel dust-press and began to make reproduction relief molded Victorian tiles. He specialized in Art Nouveau designs, which were richly glazed in typical Victorian colors. Many of his designs were produced as five tile runs for use in original and reproduction cast iron fireplaces that enjoyed a renaissance at that time. He also made some multicolored encaustic tiles. All the tiles were fired in a number of small electric kilns.

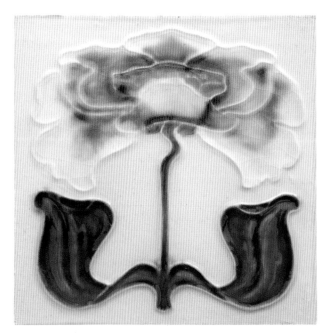

Relief molded tile with an Art Nouveau design. 6" square. 1987. This tile was produced as a glaze trial. Price group A.

Relief molded border tile with an egg and dart design. 3" x 6". 1987. This tile was produced as a glaze trial. Price group A.

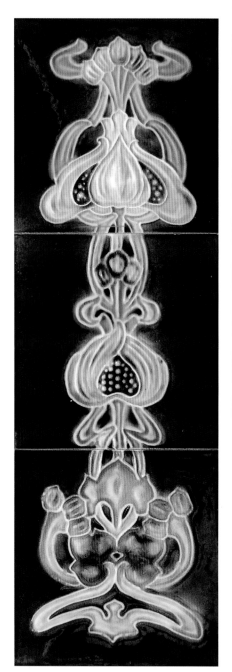

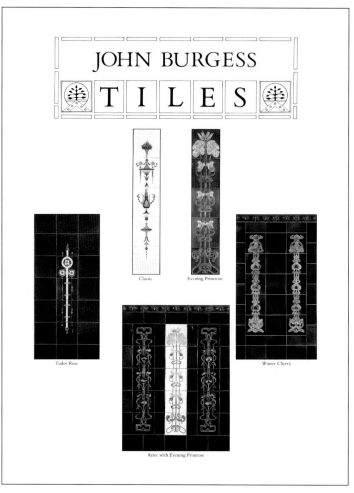

Flyer illustrating John Burgess's relief molded fireplace panel tiles in Art Nouveau style.

Panel of three relief molded tiles with an Art Nouveau design. Each tile 6" square. c.1987. Price group B.

Flyer illustrating John Burgess's relief molded tiles in Art Nouveau style.

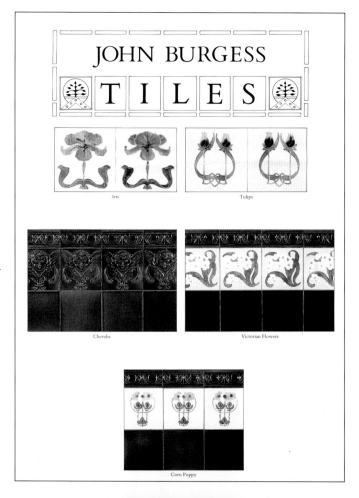

Identification and Marks

Dust pressed wall tile. 6" square. c.1983-1987.

Dust pressed wall tile. 6" square. c.1987-1995.

Alan Caiger-Smith
The Aldermaston Pottery c.1955-1993

Aldermaston, Berkshire

Alan Caiger-Smith studied painting at Camberwell School of Art in London, and history at King's College, Cambridge, before deciding to make pottery his career. He started the Aldermaston Pottery in 1955 after a short course in ceramics led by Dora Billington at the Central School of Art, London. Over the years, the Pottery had an ever-changing team of potters, usually seven or eight at a time, producing tin-glazed and luster studio pottery of the finest quality. Alan Caiger-Smith was chairman of the British Crafts Centre from 1974-1978 and was appointed a Member of the British Empire in 1988. He is the author of a number of standard works on pottery and glazes.

Although best known for his wonderful studio pottery, Alan Caiger-Smith also produced hand painted tin-glazed and luster tiles from about 1960. Most of these are painted on industrial biscuit supplied by *Candy Tiles Ltd., Hereford Tiles Ltd., H. & R. Johnson Ltd.* and others, although some small tiles were hand made from plastic clay at the pottery. The tin-glazed tiles were fired in an electric kiln and the luster tiles in the pottery's unique wood burning kiln, utilizing waste willow wood from another local industry—cricket bat manufacture.

Tiles were usually made to order and any spares or extras were sold as loose individual tiles. Site-specific tiles were sometimes made in special shapes and sizes. Although Aldermaston Pottery officially closed in 1993, Alan and his son continue to make a small number of pots and tiles.

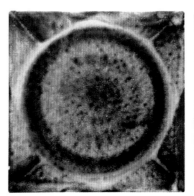

Two hand painted tin-glaze tiles with abstract designs. Each tile 4" square. 1967. Candy Tiles blanks. Price group B (each).

Hand painted tin-glaze tile with an abstract design. 6" square. 1967. Candy Tiles blank. *Courtesy of Adrian Grater.* Price group B.

Hand painted tin-glaze tile with an abstract design. 4" square. 1967. Candy Tiles blank. Price group B.

Hand painted tin-glaze tile with an abstract design. 6" square. 1967. Candy Tiles blank. *Courtesy of Adrian Grater.* Price group B.

Set of twelve plastic clay hand painted tin-glaze luster tiles with abstract designs. Each tile 2" square. c.1980. *Courtesy of Adrian Grater.* Price group E (set).

Set of twelve plastic clay hand painted tin-glaze luster tiles with abstract designs. Each tile 2" square. c.1980. *Courtesy of Adrian Grater.* Price group E (set).

Part of a panel of hand painted tin-glaze tiles with an abstract design. Each tile 4" square. c.1980. *Private collection.* Price group B (each tile).

Hand painted tin-glaze tile with an abstract design. 6" square. 1980. Shaw Hereford blank. *Courtesy of Adrian Grater.* Price group B.

Hand painted tin-glaze tile with an abstract design. 6" square. 1980. Shaw Hereford blank. *Courtesy of Adrian Grater.* Price group B.

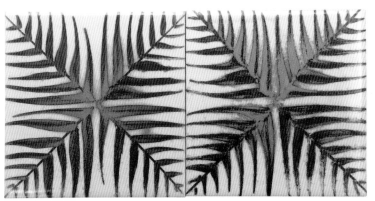

Two hand painted tin-glaze luster tiles with an abstract design. Each tile 100mm square. c.1990. H. & R. Johnson blanks. *Courtesy of Adrian Grater.* Price group B.

Identification and Marks

Hand painted signature of Alan Caiger Smith used on the backs of tiles

References

Caiger-Smith, Alan. *Lustre Pottery*. London: Faber & Faber, 1985.

Caiger-Smith, Alan. *Pottery, People & Time*. Shepton Beauchamp, Somerset: Richard Dennis Publications, 1995.

Christina Casement 1983-

Dene Cottage, West Harting, Petersfield, Hampshire

Christina Casement says about her tile making, "I know I am classed as a crafts person or 'decorator' but I consider myself an artist working on ceramic tile!" During the 1980s she created several sets of designs including ten "Jokey Pigs" and six "Elephants" as well as a number of single fruit and vegetable tiles that were sold through a tile shop in South London. In 1989, she began working for Sloane Square Tiles in London and made fewer single tiles, concentrating more on larger murals, often for use behind Aga cookers. Most of her current work is to commission only.

She hand paints her designs onto a wide variety of commercial tiles (machine and handmade) and uses on-glaze enamels, firing usually at least twice to 800°C. For a short period from 1986 to 1987, she employed a student, Samantha Bricknell.

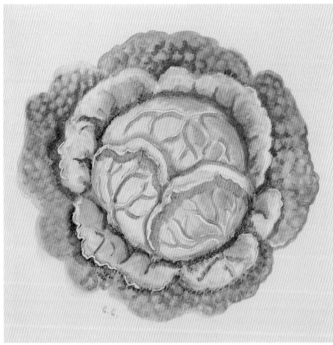

Hand painted over-glaze tile depicting a cabbage. 6" square. 1995. H. & R. Johnson blank. Price group A.

Hand painted over-glaze tile depicting a robin. 6" square. 1995. H. & R. Johnson blank. Price group A.

Set of nine hand painted over-glaze tiles depicting trees and leaves. Each tile 4" square. 1990s. Unknown commercial blanks. *Courtesy of and photograph by Christina Casement.* Price group A (each).

Set of six hand painted over-glaze tiles depicting frogs. Each tile 6" square. 1990s. H. & R. Johnson blanks. *Courtesy of and photograph by Christina Casement.* Price group A (each).

Set of four hand painted over-glaze tiles depicting fruits. Each tile 6" square. 1990s. H. & R. Johnson blanks. *Courtesy of and photograph by Christina Casement.* Price group A (each).

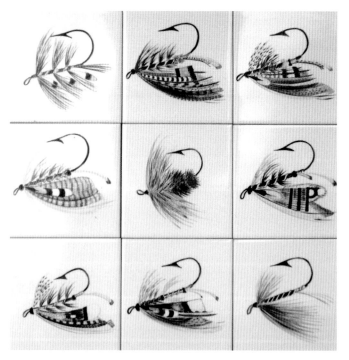

Set of nine hand painted over-glaze tiles depicting fishing flies. Each tile 6" square. 1990s. H. & R. Johnson blanks. *Courtesy of and photograph by Christina Casement.* Price group A (each).

Panel of nine hand painted over-glaze tiles depicting a cockerel. Each tile 100mm square. 1990s. H. & R. Johnson blanks. *Courtesy of and photograph by Christina Casement.* Price group C (panel).

Set of six hand painted over-glaze tiles depicting Punch & Judy. Each tile 6" square. 1990s. H. & R. Johnson blanks. *Courtesy of and photograph by Christina Casement.* Price group C (panel).

Hand painted over-glaze tile depicting a "Barn Owl." 6" square. 1999. H. & R. Johnson blank. *Courtesy of and photograph by Christina Casement.* Price group A.

Many of Christina Casement's tiles are signed with her initials, "CC" or "C Casement," or her full name.

Self-adhesive label on H. & R. Johnson 6" square blank. 1990s.

Hand painted over-glaze tile depicting a "Rosemarinus Officinalis." 6" square. c.1999. H. & R. Johnson blank. *Courtesy of and photograph by Christina Casement.* Price group A.

Chelsea Pottery 1952-1997

1952-1994: Radnor Walk, Chelsea, London
1994-1997: Ebury Mews, Chelsea, London

Chelsea Pottery was established in 1952 by David and Mary Rawnsley as an "open studio," a place where any potter could come and work. They also held lessons and classes for amateur potters. In 1959, the Rawnsleys retired and left the Pottery in the hands of Brian Hubbard, who continued to run Chelsea Pottery until its closure in 1997.

The tile makers at Chelsea Pottery seem to have employed two techniques—conventional hand painting and a very distinctive technique: effectively sgraffito using colored glazes heavily applied to red or buff bodied floor tiles. These were supplied by *Carter & Co.* or *George Woolliscroft & Son*, whilst white and buff wall tiles were supplied by *Hereford Tiles Ltd., H. & E. Smith Ltd.*, and occasionally *H. & R. Johnson Ltd.*.

From the early 1970s, several important tile makers worked at the Pottery, including Francisca Blackburne, Audrey Durnan, Joyce Morgan, Christina Sheppard, and a number of other artists whose signatures have not been identified. Several of these went on to establish studios of their own after leaving Chelsea Pottery.

Identification and Marks

This mark was used together with individual signatures as shown on following pages.

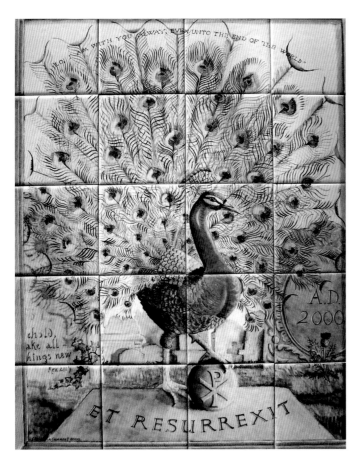

Panel of twenty hand painted over-glaze tiles depicting a peacock. Each tile 100mm square. 1999. H. & R. Johnson blanks. *Courtesy of and photograph by Christina Casement.* Price group C (panel).

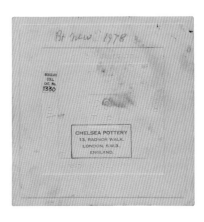

Rubber stamp mark on a Hereford Tiles 6" square blank. c.1975-1990. This tile 1978.

Jane Francisca Blackburne
Chelsea Pottery 1984-1988
Francisca Ceramica 1988-1997

1988-1997: Stratton Close, Hill Farm Lane, Chalfont St. Giles, Buckinghamshire

Jane Francisca Blackburne spent much of her childhood traveling with her family and spent her formative years in Naples, returning as an adult to work in Rome. Following her mother's example, she painted and drew from an early age and studied Art and the History of Art at Oxford before attending the Ceramics Department of Amersham College, Buckinghamshire. From 1984 to 1988, she was a principal decorator for the Chelsea Pottery, during which time her work was displayed in a number of top stores in London and abroad. On February 29, 1988, she started her own ceramic business, which she named after her Spanish paternal grandmother, producing a range of decorative tiles—both standard designs and specials to commission—and commemorative bowls for weddings, christenings, birthdays, and retirements. Among her large commissions was a 15' x 30' tile panel for the AIWA electronics company headquarters in Wales. In 1997, she moved to Brighton in Sussex and did a degree course in 3D design. At that time, she turned from pottery to sculpture and no longer makes tiles. More recently she returned to Italy to live.

Francisca's work is mainly floral, although she also produced a range of 6" square animal tiles. Her early tiles during the Chelsea Pottery days were produced on *H. & E. Smith Ltd.* blanks and her later work under Francisca Ceramica was done on *H. & R. Johnson Ltd.* blanks. Her tiles were painted in-glaze on a tin-glaze base, often with sgraffito details, and were fired in an electric kiln to 1080°C in an oxidizing atmosphere.

Hand painted and sgraffito tile with a floral design. 4¼" square. c.1990. H. & R. Johnson blank. Francisca Ceramica period. Price group A.

Hand painted and sgraffito tile with a floral design. 6" across. c.1985. H. & E. Smith blank. Chelsea Pottery period (marked on back). Price group B.

Hand painted and sgraffito tile with a floral design. 4¼" square. c.1990. H. & R. Johnson blank. Francisca Ceramica period. Price group A.

Identification and Marks

Sgraffito or painted mark on
face of tile. 1984-1997.

Tiles from the Chelsea Pottery period also have the rectangular Chelsea Pottery rubber stamp mark.

Audrey Durnan
Chelsea Pottery 1965-1972
Shawnigan Lake Pottery, Vancouver Island, Canada 1972-
1990
Claremont, California, USA 1990-

Audrey Durnan was born in Canterbury, Kent and trained for four years as an artist at the Canterbury College of Art, where she specialized in sculpture and pottery. After graduation in 1965, she worked for Chelsea Pottery, where she designed and painted floral designs on pots and tiles. Whilst at Chelsea, she designed and made Sunflower tiles for the Chelsea Potter Public House on the corner of Radnor Walk, close to the Pottery, and a heraldic panel for Viscount Monkton of Bletchley in Buckinghamshire.

In 1972, she emigrated to Canada and established the Shawnigan Lake Pottery on Vancouver Island, where she continued to make similar pots and tiles. She now resides in Southern California, where she has been designing pottery and creating decoupage plates and eggs. In recent years, this has been curtailed due to the onset of arthritis but she has been studying the art of silk painting and now produces wonderfully vibrant silk scarves and cushions.

Hand painted and sgraffito tile with a floral design. 8" square in original frame. c.1975. Unknown commercial blank. *Private collection.* Price group B.

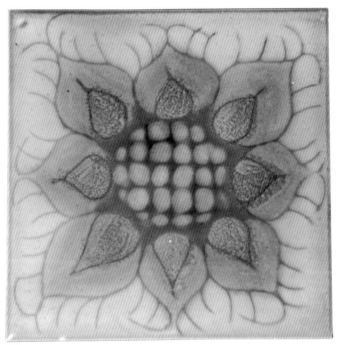

Hand painted tile depicting a stylized flower. 6" square. c.1970. Hereford Tiles blank. *Courtesy of Audrey Durnan, photograph by Robert Woods.* Price group B.

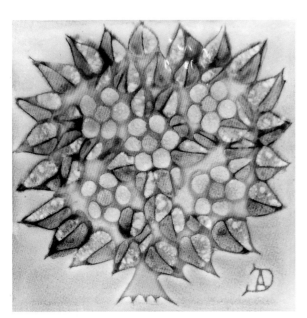

Hand painted and sgraffito tile with a floral design. 6" square. c.1972. Hereford Tiles blank. *Courtesy of Douglas van der Horst.* Price group B.

Hand painted tile depicting a stylized flower. 6" square. c.1970. Hereford Tiles blank. *Courtesy of Audrey Durnan, photograph by Robert Woods.* Price group B.

Hand painted tile with a nine-fold floral design. 6" square. c.1970. Hereford Tiles blank. *Courtesy of Audrey Durnan, photograph by Robert Woods.* Price group B.

Hand painted tile with a stylized floral design. 6" square. c.1970. Hereford Tiles blank. *Courtesy of Audrey Durnan, photograph by Robert Woods.* Price group B.

Hand painted tile with a stylized floral design. 6" square. c.1970. Hereford Tiles blank. *Courtesy of Audrey Durnan, photograph by Robert Woods.* Price group B.

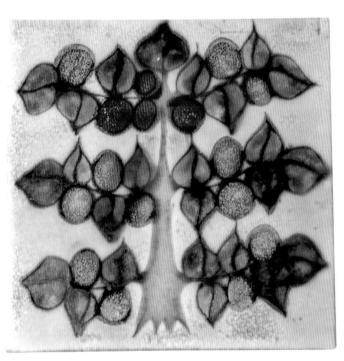

Hand painted tile depicting a stylized "Orange Tree." 6" square. c.1970. Hereford Tiles blank. *Courtesy of Audrey Durnan, photograph by Robert Woods.* Price group B.

Hand painted tile with a stylized floral design. 6" diameter. 1971. H. & R. Johnson blank. *Courtesy of Audrey Durnan, photograph by Robert Woods.* Price group B.

Sgraffito mark on face of tile.
1965-1972.

Tiles from the Chelsea Pottery period also have the rectangular Chelsea Pottery rubber stamp mark. Tiles made at the Shawnigan Lake Pottery are marked with their name on the back.

Joyce Morgan

Hand painted tile with a stylized floral design. 6" diameter. 1971. H. & R. Johnson blank. *Courtesy of Audrey Durnan, photograph by Robert Woods.* Price group B.

Hand painted and sgraffito tile depicting an owl. 6" square. c.1972. Carter & Co. red body floor tile blank. Price group B.

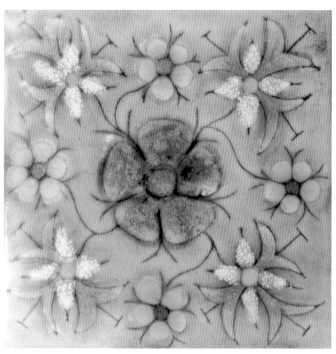

Hand painted tile with a stylized floral design. 6" square. c.1970. Hereford Tiles blank. *Courtesy of Audrey Durnan, photograph by Robert Woods.* Price group B.

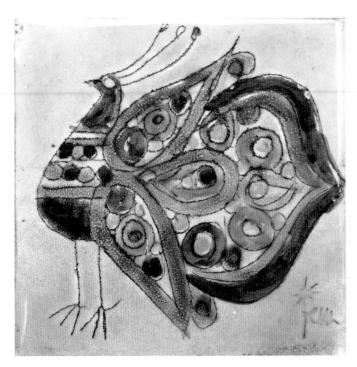

Hand painted and sgraffito tile depicting a peacock. 6" square. c.1972. Unknown commercial blank. *Courtesy of Adrian Grater.* Price group B.

Identification and Marks

Sgraffito mark on face of tile. 1970s.

Christina Sheppard c.1960-c.1985
Chelsea Pottery c.1960-c.1975
624 Fulham Road, London c.1975-c.1985

Born in England in 1931, Christina Sheppard and her parents moved to Paris in 1937 where her mother, a sculptress, took her to draw from the nude in a life class. The war brought them back to England and Oxford, and at school, Christina remembers that Art and English were the only subjects taught properly, so that she excelled in little else. In 1950, she joined the Illustration Department at Camberwell School of Art, under Edward Ardizzone. Her initial efforts as a freelance illustrator brought her a commission from the publishers Faber & Faber, but being very shy and under-confident

she became so lonely working on her own that she joined Chelsea Pottery for a short time as a designer.

Marriage and children followed, with a gap in her working life until she began designing again in the early 1960s—this time tiles. Her designs were accepted by the Design Centre and sold through Harrods and Heals, as well as craft shops in London and the provinces. Her tiles were also sold in stores as far afield as New York, Amsterdam, Paris, and Tokyo but she specially enjoyed working with private commissions for fireplaces and bathrooms. Her major commissions included a large mural for the Shakespeare Centre in Stratford-on-Avon and a panel illustrating the production methods of cider for a cider company in Hereford. Some of Christina's tiles are also included in the permanent collections of the Victoria & Albert Museum and were on display in the Ceramics Department.

Christina specialized in hand painted tiles with additional sgraffito decoration and particularly liked landscapes. She also did a series of Russian-style saints and a few animals. All her tiles were painted on red-bodied floor tiles, mainly from *George Woolliscroft & Son*. She also painted a few 9" x 6" designs on red clay roofing tiles. Christina stopped making tiles in the mid-1980s to concentrate on book illustration and landscape painting.

Hand painted and sgraffito tile depicting a cockerel. 6" square. 1973. George Woolliscroft & Son Ironstone floor tile blank. Price group B.

Hand painted and sgraffito tile depicting a saint on horseback. 6" square. 1974. George Woolliscroft & Son Ironstone floor tile blank. Price group B.

Hand painted and sgraffito tile depicting a rural scene. 6" square. 1976. George Woolliscroft & Son Ironstone floor tile blank. Price group B.

Hand painted and sgraffito tile depicting a king on horseback. 6" square. 1974. George Woolliscroft & Son Ironstone floor tile blank. Price group B.

Hand painted and sgraffito tile depicting a rural river scene. 6" square. 1976. George Woolliscroft & Son Ironstone floor tile blank. Price group B.

Hand painted and sgraffito tile depicting an owl. 6" square. 1984. George Woolliscroft & Son Ironstone floor tile blank. *Courtesy of Roger Hensman.* Price group B.

Hand painted and sgraffito tile depicting a scene through a window. 6" square. 1985. George Woolliscroft & Son Ironstone floor tile blank. Price group B.

Hand painted and sgraffito tile depicting a snow scene. 6" square. 1980s. Unknown commercial blank. *Courtesy of and photograph by Christina Sheppard.* Price group B.

Hand painted and sgraffito tile depicting a cat on a windowsill. 6" square. 1980s. Unknown commercial blank. *Courtesy of and photograph by Christina Sheppard.* Price group B.

Hand painted and sgraffito tile depicting a stylized swan. 6" x 10½". 1980s. Unknown roof tile blank. Christina Sheppard occasionally used roof tiles for her larger pieces. *Courtesy of and photograph by Christina Sheppard.* Price group C.

Hand painted and sgraffito tile depicting a farm. 6" square. 1980s. Unknown commercial blank. *Courtesy of and photograph by Christina Sheppard.* Price group B.

Relief molded plastic clay tile depicting an exotic bird. 6" square. 1980s. *Courtesy of and photograph by Christina Sheppard.* Price group B.

Six hand painted and sgraffito tiles depicting processes in the manufacture of cider. Each tile 6" square. 1980s. Unknown commercial blanks. *Courtesy of and photograph by Christina Sheppard.* Price group B (each).

Relief molded plastic clay plaque depicting a ram. 7" x 6". 1980s. *Courtesy of and photograph by Christina Sheppard.* Price group B.

Four slip trailed tiles with pseudo medieval designs. Each tile 6" square. 1980s. Unknown commercial blanks. *Courtesy of and photograph by Christina Sheppard.* Price group B (each).

Identification and Marks

Sgraffito mark on face of tile. c.1960-c.1985.

Unidentified Artists

Hand painted and sgraffito tile depicting an iris. 6″ square. 1978. Hereford Tiles blank. Signed with an indecipherable signature on the front. Price group B.

Hand painted and sgraffito tile depicting a stylized flower. 6″ square. 1973. Unknown commercial blank. Signed "JB73" on front. *Courtesy of Adrian Grater.* Price group B.

Hand painted and sgraffito tile depicting a sunflower. 6″ square. 1966. Richards Tiles blank. Signed with an indecipherable signature on the front. Price group B.

Hand painted and sgraffito tile with a floral design. 6" square. 1984. H. & E. Smith blank. Signed "JG" on front. *Courtesy of Roger Hensman.* Price group B.

Identification and Marks

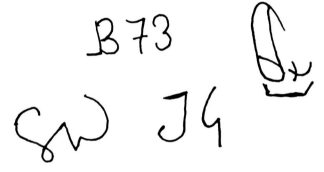

A selection of sgraffito marks found on the face of Chelsea Pottery tiles. c.1952-c.1997.

Caroline Chouler
Caroline Chouler Ceramics 1996-

79 Corbar Road, Buxton, Derbyshire

Until 1996, Caroline Chouler had been making small whimsical sculptures in ceramic. In the spring of that year she made her first miniature tiles, approximately 1¾" square with an added decorative hanger. Her tiles are hand made from very white grogged earthenware clay, rolled, cut, carved, and modeled. Further decoration is added by printing or incising, and occasionally the tiles are press molded or sprigged. Oxides and under-glaze colors are added and a porcelain slip is used for further color and texture. Depending on the design, the tiles are glazed with a colored earthenware glaze or a transparent crackle glaze to give a layered watercolor effect. The tiles are biscuit fired to 1100°C and glost fired to 1040°C; a third firing at a lower temperature is sometimes used for further decoration.

For a time, Caroline employed a student from Chesterfield College, Richard Shore, who went on to study at Nottingham University.

Panel of small hand carved and molded tiles depicting scenes from Buxton in Derbyshire. *Courtesy of and photograph by Caroline Chouler.* Price group E (panel).

Detail from a large panel of hand painted plastic clay tiles depicting an ocean mural. *Courtesy of and photograph by Caroline Chouler.*

C J Chouler or Caroline. J Chouler

A selection of painted marks used on the face of tiles.

Lubna Chowdhary 1998-

162 Sunnyhill Road, London SW16

Lubna Chowdhray's vividly glazed tiles are produced as a standard range and also as specials. She uses biscuit purchased from *Clayworth Potteries* and *H. & E. Smith Ltd.*, these being cut to a special size for her. She also produces her own handmade press-molded blanks on occasion. All are decorated using low temperature glazes applied on a turntable or brushed.

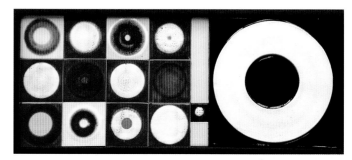

Panel of hand decorated tiles with an abstract design entitled "Collect1." Various sizes. *Courtesy of and photograph by Lubna Chowdhary.* Price group D (panel).

Ten individual hand molded "tiles with loops." Various sizes. *Courtesy of and photograph by Caroline Chouler.* Price group A (each).

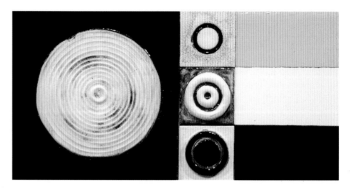

Panel of hand decorated tiles with an abstract design entitled "Cooker." Various sizes. *Courtesy of and photograph by Lubna Chowdhary.* Price group C (panel).

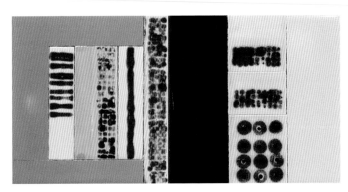

Panel of hand decorated tiles with an abstract design entitled "Orange." Various sizes. *Courtesy of and photograph by Lubna Chowdhary.* Price group C (panel).

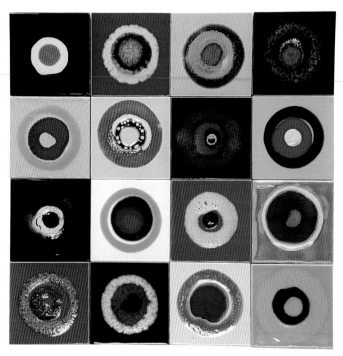

Panel of sixteen hand decorated tiles with circular abstract designs. Each tile 2" square. *Courtesy of and photograph by Lubna Chowdhary.* Price group C (panel).

Lubna Chowdhary's tiles in situ at St George's Hospital hydro-therapy pool. *Courtesy of and photograph by Lubna Chowdhary.*

Identification and Marks
No identifying marks.

Pauline Clements
Pulhams Mill Studio 1979-

Pulhams Mill Studio, Brompton Regis, Nr. Dulverton, Somerset

Pauline Clements was born in Chailey, Sussex in 1950 and moved to Sydney, Australia in 1959, where she attended art school before obtaining her first job in an art studio in Paddington, a suburb of Sydney. There she discovered an interest in ceramics and designed a number of tiles illustrating local scenes, wildlife, and flowers. In 1979, she returned to England with her husband, Ian Mawby, and they set about renovating Pulhams Mill on Exmoor in Somerset, turning it into a craft centre.

Pauline has illustrated a number of books for the National Trust and others, and has established a successful business making hand painted bone china mugs and tea sets. She also produces silk-screen printed tiles, some of which have additional hand coloring, and a small range of entirely hand painted designs. Her tile designs feature many of the animals and birds found on Exmoor and elsewhere in the U.K., and topographical scenes produced for specific locations. All are produced on *H. & R. Johnson Ltd.* blanks. Her husband, Ian, produces furniture made from English hardwoods.

Hand screen printed tile depicting "Norfolk Plover, Birds of East Anglia." 6" square. 1981. H. & R. Johnson blank. Price group A.

Hand screen printed tile depicting "Chatsworth House, Derbyshire." 6" square in original cork trivet. 1998. H. & R. Johnson blank. Price group A.

Hand screen printed tile depicting "Wells Cathedral, Somerset steps leading to the Chapter House." 6" square. 1999. H. & R. Johnson blank. Price group A.

Hand screen printed design trial (on paper) depicting "Lincoln Cathedral." 6" square. *Courtesy of Pauline Clements*. Price group A.

Margery Clinton
Margery Clinton Ceramics 1961-

1961-1995: The Pottery, Newton Port, Haddington, East Lothian, Scotland
1995- : 2 Templelands, 29 High Street, Dunbar, East Lothian, Scotland

Margery Clinton's specialty has always been luster tiles, but over the years she has also produced a wide range of tube-lined, hand painted, and screen printed tiles for special commissions. William de Morgan's ruby luster tiles inspire her main range and these she faithfully recreates, using the original techniques of reduction firing pioneered by de Morgan in the 1860s and 1870s. These were mainly sold through *Kenneth Clark Ceramics* at Lewes, Sussex and are now available through The Tile Factory (see *Amabis Tiles*). She decorates mainly on *H. & R. Johnson Ltd.* blanks.

Hand screen printed design trial (on paper) depicting "Jamaica Inn, Bodmin Moor, Cornwall." 6" square. *Courtesy of Pauline Clements*. Price group A.

Hand painted tile with a floral design. 6" square. c.1980. H. & R. Johnson blank. *Courtesy of Hans van Lemmen*. Price group B.

Identification and Marks

In-print signature used on most of Pauline Clements' tiles.

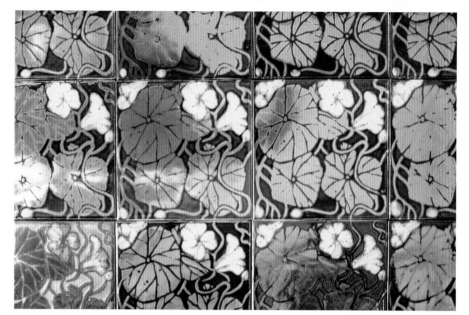

Detail of a panel of hand screen printed luster tiles with a floral design. Each tile 6" square. 1990s. H. & R. Johnson blanks. *Courtesy of and photograph by Margery Clinton.* Price group A (each tile).

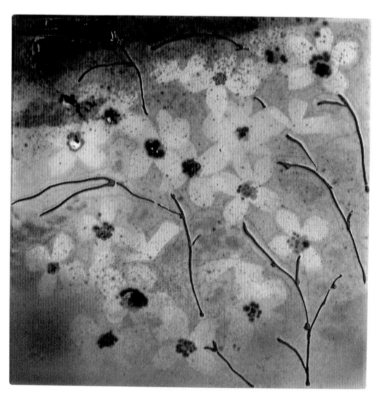

Hand painted tile with a floral design. 6" square. 1990s. H. & R. Johnson blank. *Courtesy of and photograph by Margery Clinton.* Price group B.

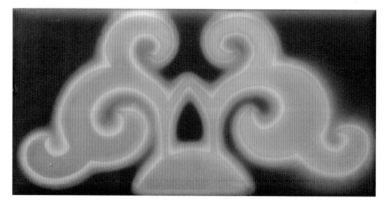

Hand screen printed luster tile with an abstract design. 3" x 6". 1990s. H. & R. Johnson blank. Price group A.

Hand screen printed luster tile depicting a galleon, based on an original design by William de Morgan. 6" square. 1990s. H. & R. Johnson blank. *Courtesy of Carolyn Wraight.* Price group B.

Hand screen printed luster tile depicting a pelican, based on an original design by William de Morgan. 6" square. 1990s. H. & R. Johnson blank. *Courtesy of and photograph by Margery Clinton.* Price group B.

Hand screen printed luster tile depicting a mythical bird, based on an original design by William de Morgan. 6" square. 1990s. H. & R. Johnson blank. *Courtesy of and photograph by Margery Clinton.* Price group B.

Identification and Marks

Rubber stamp mark on H. & R. Johnson 3" x 6" blank. 1990s.

Stephen Cocker 1983-

Bedale, North Yorkshire

The gift of two old Dutch delft tiles was the starting point of Stephen Cocker's interest in tile-making. He was so impressed with them that he set about learning the techniques involved and experimented until he could produce his own hand-made tiles. Stephen designs his tiles to have a "delft" feel to them but with modern-day motifs. Among his most popular designs are a series of tiles entitled "Cosmos," featuring the moon, sun, and stars in an updated delft-style border. This series was sold extensively through the retail shops of *Fired Earth* until about 2000. Since that time, Stephen has produced fewer tiles and now concentrates on making wall plaques, but continues to use the tin-glaze technique.

Stephen makes his own biscuit and also creates all the glazes and pigments himself. He fires the tiles in an electric kiln. At the height of his business, he was producing upwards of a thousand tiles a week.

Hand painted and sgraffito plastic clay tile depicting jugs. 6" square. c.1996. *Courtesy of Hans van Lemmen.* Price group B.

Hand painted and sgraffito plastic clay tile depicting a fish. 6" square. c.1996. *Courtesy of Hans van Lemmen.* Price group B.

Identification and Marks
No identifying marks.

Jean M. Cook
The Tile Makers 1992-

The Tannery, Chapel Lane, Ellel, Lancashire
Greaves Cottage, Conder Green Road, Galgate, Nr Lancaster

Jean Cook established The Tile Makers in 1992 to produce hand painted, press-molded relief tiles. Her tiles are cleverly designed with individual elements that can be arranged in many different ways to create continuous patterns or panels. In addition, she produced a range of spot feature tiles and small tile panels.

High relief press molded plastic clay tile depicting strawberries. 4" square. 1990s. *Courtesy of Jean M. Cook.* Price group A.

The white earthenware tiles are biscuit fired to 1080°C, painted in under-glaze colors, and re-fired. They are then enamel painted over-glaze and fired a third time. A fingerprint is impressed into the back of the tile to identify the person who pressed the tile. A small painted spider mark is also used on occasion.

Jean has now virtually ceased manufacturing her own tiles, and concentrates on selling her designs to other tile makers.

High relief press molded plastic clay tile depicting grapes. 4" square. 1990s. Price group A.

High relief press molded plastic clay tile depicting an apple. 4" square. 1990s. *Courtesy of Jean M. Cook.* Price group A.

High relief press molded plastic clay tile depicting a butterfly. 4" square. 1990s. Price group A.

High relief press molded plastic clay tile depicting blackberries. 4" square. 1990s. *Courtesy of Jean M. Cook.* Price group A.

High relief press molded plastic clay tile depicting sunflowers. 4" x 8". 1990s. Price group A.

Composite panel of high relief press molded plastic clay tiles depicting clematis. Each tile 4" square. 1990s. *Courtesy of and photograph by Jean M. Cook.* Price group C (panel).

Identification and Marks

Most of The Tilemaker's Tiles are marked with a fingerprint on the back; in addition, some tiles also carry this "spider" mark. 1992-

High relief press molded plastic clay tile depicting sunflowers. 4" x 8". 1990s. Price group A.

Set of five high relief press molded plastic clay tiles, "Pear Swag." Each tile 4" square. 1990s. Price group B (set).

Chris Cox
Treamlod Pottery 1992-1994
Treamlod Tilery 1995-1997
The Encaustic Tile Co. 1997-2001
Amalgamated with Craven Dunnill Jackfield Ltd. 2001-

1992-1997: Springwells, Amblestone, Haverfordwest, Pembrokeshire, Wales
1997-2001: Jackfield Tile Museum, Ironbridge, Telford, Shropshire
2001- : Craven Dunnill Jackfield Ltd, Jackfield Tile Museum, Ironbridge, Telford, Shropshire

Chris Cox's interest in tiles was first aroused during his time at university. When he left, he set up his own small pottery in a workshop in the garden of his parent's home. There he developed a range of household pottery and experimented with producing encaustic tiles that he began to make commercially in 1992. Demand became so great that by 1997 Chris had outgrown his original premises and moved to a larger workshop within the former Craven Dunnill tile factory, now part of the Ironbridge Gorge Museum near Telford in Shropshire. In February 2001, the business was bought by *Craven Dunnill Jackfield Ltd*. and Chris Cox continues as manager of their encaustic tile department. He is now recognized as the country's leading maker of encaustic tiles.

When Chris first started making tiles, very little was known about the techniques used by Victorian manufacturers to create multicolored encaustic tiles. He had to develop his own clay recipes and undertook hundreds of experiments to successfully recreate the palette of colors used in the 19th century. He also needed to overcome the problem of differential shrinkage of the colored clays, but was eventually able to produce tiles equal in quality to the originals. In addition to copying traditional patterns, Chris has also developed designs of his own and will undertake to design to commission. Chris's tiles are much in demand for the restoration of Victorian churches, civic buildings, and Victorian homes, as well as for new construction.

Glazed plastic clay encaustic tile with a double bird design based on a medieval original. 6" square. 1994. Price group B.

Unglazed plastic clay encaustic tile with a border design based on a Victorian original. 2" x 6". 1994. Price group B.

Unglazed plastic clay three-color encaustic tile with a border design based on a Victorian original. 6" square. 1994. Price group B.

Glazed plastic clay encaustic tile with a griffin design based on a medieval original. 6" square. 1994. Price group B.

Unglazed plastic clay three-color encaustic tile with a neo-gothic design based on a Victorian original. 6″ square. 1994. Price group B.

Glazed plastic clay encaustic tile with a fleur-de-lis design. 3″ square. 1994. Price group A.

Glazed plastic clay encaustic tile with a heraldic design. 6″ x 4″. 1994. Price group B.

Unglazed plastic clay six-color encaustic tile with a heraldic design. 6"
square. 1994. Price group B.

Glazed plastic clay encaustic tile with a geometric design based on a
medieval original from Penn in Buckinghamshire. 6" square. 1994. Price
group B.

Glazed plastic clay encaustic tile with a heraldic lions design. 6" square.
1994. Price group B.

Glazed plastic clay five-color encaustic tile with a neo-gothic design based on a Victorian original. 6" square. 1997. *Courtesy of Chris Cox.* Price group B.

Unglazed plastic clay three-color encaustic tile with a neo-gothic design based on a Victorian original. 6" square. 1994. Price group B.

Glazed plastic clay five-color encaustic tile with a neo-gothic design based on a Victorian original. 4" square. 1995. *Courtesy of Chris Cox.* Price group B.

Glazed plastic clay five-color encaustic tile with a neo-gothic design based on a Victorian original. 6″ square. 1995. Price group B.

Detail of geometric pavement including plastic clay encaustic tiles. Center tile 6″ square. 1997. *Courtesy of Chris & Michelle Cox.* Price group B (each decorated tile).

Identification and Marks

Impressed mark of the letters "TP" designed to look like a small jug or pitcher, used from 1991 to February 1994. The Treamlod Pottery's first products were jugs but this mark was also used on early encaustic tiles.

TREAMLOD POTTERY

Impressed mark used from 1992 to February 1994, often in conjunction with the jug mark.

Impressed mark used on 6″ square tiles from February 1994 to October 1995. Often used with a date stamp as in this example. This tile September 6, 1994.

Impressed mark used on tiles up to 4¼″ square from October 1995 to 1996, sometimes in conjunction with a date stamp.

Combined impressed marks used from 1996 to 1997. The small dust-pressed mark with the initials "TT" was also used on its own on smaller tiles. This tile 12 August 12, 1996 (date stamped).

Impressed maker's mark used on some tiles made by Chris Cox. 1996-1997.

Impressed maker's mark used on some tiles made by Benjamin Campbell Grey. 1996-1997.

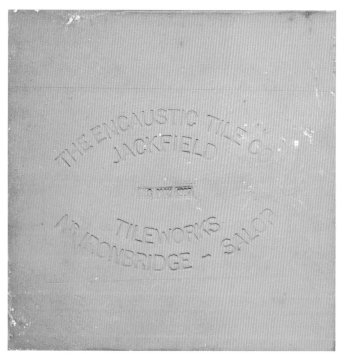

Impressed mark used from 1997 to 2001, often in conjunction with a date stamp. This tile May 8, 1997.

Impressed mark used on tiles made for Fired Earth, c.1998 to 2000. 3" square. 1999 (19 July).

Terry Curran 1984-

Chapel Street, Mosborough, Sheffield, South Yorkshire

Terry Curran's tiles are unique one-twelfth scale replicas of original Victorian and Edwardian designs and are made in exactly the same way as their full size counterparts: printed, hand painted, or relief molded. The detail incorporated makes it difficult to realize from a photograph that they are only half an inch across! The tiles are even scale thickness, making them truly authentic in appearance when used in a doll's house or architectural model.

Terry uses a modified earthenware body cut by hand; it is biscuit-fired, then decorated and glost fired in a small electric kiln. He also produces a range of two-inch diameter tiles for setting into spirit flasks produced by a local Sheffield pewter firm.

Panel of twelve relief molded plastic clay miniature tiles with traditional Victorian designs. Each tile ½" square. 1990s. *Courtesy of Terry Curran.* Price group A (panel).

Panel of twelve screen printed plastic clay miniature tiles with traditional Dutch designs. Each tile ½" square. 1990s. *Courtesy of Terry Curran.* Price group A (panel).

Composite panel of thirty-three screen printed plastic clay miniature floor tiles with traditional encaustic designs. Each tile ½″ square. 1990s. *Courtesy of Terry Curran*. Price group B (panel).

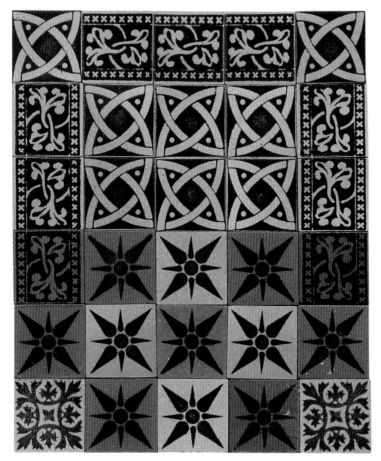

Composite panel of thirty screen printed plastic clay miniature floor tiles with traditional encaustic designs. Each tile ½″ square. 1990s. *Courtesy of Terry Curran*. Price group B (panel).

Composite panel of sixty-four screen printed plastic clay miniature floor tiles with traditional encaustic designs. Each tile ½″ square. 1990s. *Courtesy of Terry Curran*. Price group B (panel).

Eight miniature round tiles in a variety of techniques. ½" and 5/8" diameter. 1990s. *Courtesy of Terry Curran.* Price group A (each).

Six miniature round relief molded tiles with Celtic knot designs. Each tile 2" diameter. 1990s. *Courtesy of Terry Curran.* Price group A (each).

Two miniature slabbed fireplaces with hand mottled tiles. Each fireplace 4" wide. 1990s. *Courtesy of and photograph by Terry Curran.* Price group B (each fireplace).

Identification and Marks
No identifying marks.

John & Fiona Cutting
Withersdale Tiles 1970-1988

Withersdale Cross, Harleston, Norfolk

In 1970, John and Fiona Cutting were looking for tiles to decorate a newly installed kitchen in their home. Unable to find tiles that appealed to them, they decided to experiment with making their own, especially as John had some experience working with a potter. After about a year of experimentation, they were able to produce their first commercial tiles—beginning with a series of insect designs that were painted onto biscuit tile and glazed with an alkaline glaze. They also produced a range of hand painted delft tiles using cobalt and manganese oxides on tin-glaze.

Screen printed and hand colored tile depicting a shellduck, designed by Fiona Cutting. 4¼" square. c.1970. Hereford Tiles blank. Price group A.

In 1972-73, they introduced their most popular series, "British Birds," and a similar range of "Small Animals." Initially these were hand painted, but in 1976-77 they started to use screen-printed outlines colored with translucent glazes. A series of "Aesop's Fables" was introduced in 1976 and in 1982 they produced a number of designs based on the engravings of Thomas Bewick and others. Also during the 1980s, they introduced a range of screen printed and hand painted abstract designs. A further development was the introduction of ceramic clocks, produced as single unframed tiles, and single and double framed tiles fitted with a quartz clock movement. All their tiles were decorated on biscuit bought in from *H. & R. Johnson Ltd.* and *Hereford Tiles Ltd.*

By 1988, John and Fiona's enthusiasm for decorative tiles had waned and they moved to South Wales where they now run a successful sailing holiday business.

Screen printed and hand colored tile depicting a robin, designed by Fiona Cutting. 4¼″ square. c.1970. Hereford Tiles blank. Price group A.

Screen printed and hand colored tile depicting a kingfisher, designed by Fiona Cutting. 4¼″ square in original mahogany frame. c.1970. Hereford Tiles blank. Price group A.

Screen printed and hand colored tile depicting a wren, designed by Fiona Cutting. 4¼″ square in original mahogany frame. c.1970. Hereford Tiles blank. Price group A.

Screen printed and hand colored tile depicting a cormorant, designed by Fiona Cutting. 4¼″ square. c.1970. Hereford Tiles blank. Price group A.

Screen printed and hand colored tile depicting a magpie, designed by Fiona Cutting. 4¼" square. c.1972. Hereford Tiles blank. Price group A.

Screen printed and hand colored tile depicting "Marsh Marigolds," designed and signed by Fiona Cutting (one in a series of three). 6" diameter in original frame. c.1975. H. & R. Johnson blank. Price group A.

Screen printed and hand colored tile depicting a heron, designed and signed by John Cutting (no. 5 in a series of eight). 6" square in original frame. c.1972. Hereford Tiles blank. Price group A.

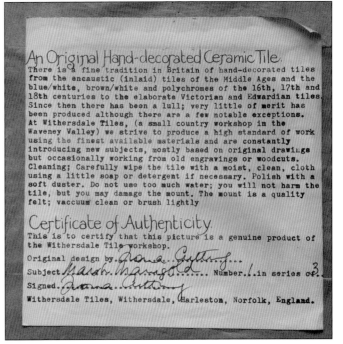

Label on the back of "Marsh Marigolds," designed and signed by Fiona Cutting (one in a series of three).

Screen printed and hand colored tile depicting Canada geese, designed and signed by John Cutting (one in a series of eight). 6" diameter. c.1975. H. & R. Johnson blank. Price group A.

Screen printed and hand colored tile depicting swans, designed by Fiona Cutting. 4¼" square in original frame. c.1975. Hereford Tiles blank. *Courtesy of Paul & Angela Pitkin.* Price group A.

Screen printed tile depicting "Pisces," designed by Fiona Cutting. 6" square. c.1975. Price group A.

Screen printed and hand colored tile depicting "The crow and the pitcher – Aesop," from a series of Aesop's Fables. 6" square. 1977. H. & R. Johnson blank. *Courtesy of Freddie & Annie Taggart.* Price group A.

Screen printed and hand colored tile depicting a bull, designed and signed by John Cutting. 6" square. 1975. H. & R. Johnson blank. *Courtesy of Freddie & Annie Taggart.* Price group A.

Screen printed and hand colored tile depicting "The raven and the swan – Aesop," from a series of Aesop's Fables. 6" square. 1977. H. & R. Johnson blank. *Courtesy of Freddie & Annie Taggart.* Price group A.

Screen printed and hand colored tile depicting a hare. 4¼″ square. 1977. H. & R. Johnson blank. *Courtesy of Freddie & Annie Taggart.* Price group A.

Screen printed and hand colored tile depicting a horse. 6″ square. 1975. H. & R. Johnson blank. Price group A.

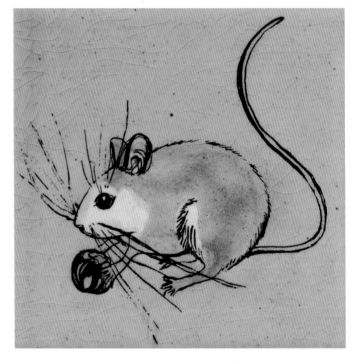

Screen printed and hand colored tile depicting a field-mouse. 4¼″ square. 1980. H. & R. Johnson blank. *Courtesy of Freddie & Annie Taggart.* Price group A.

Screen printed and hand colored tile depicting a pheasant. 6"
square. c.1977. H. & R. Johnson blank. Price group A.

Screen printed and hand colored tile depicting horse trials. 4" x 6". 1980. H. & R. Johnson
blank. *Courtesy of Freddie & Annie Taggart*. Price group A.

Screen printed and hand colored tile
depicting "Sedan Chair." 6" square.
1977. H. & R. Johnson blank.
Courtesy of Freddie & Annie Taggart.
Price group A.

Screen printed and hand colored tile depicting harvest. 6" square. 1977. H. & R. Johnson blank. *Courtesy of Freddie & Annie Taggart.* Price group A.

Screen printed and hand colored tile depicting a family of rabbits. 6" square in original cardboard packaging. 1977. H. & R. Johnson blank. Price group A.

Hand screen printed flyer for the Withersdale cats series, designed by Fiona Cutting. c.1975. Price group A (each tile).

Front of original cardboard packaging, closed.

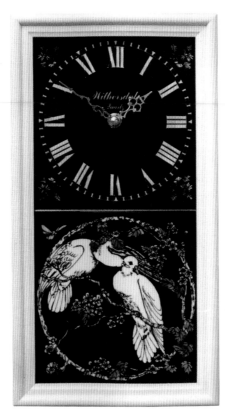

Promotional photograph illustrating three Withersdale tile clocks. Two 6" tiles in pine frames. c.1979. *Courtesy of Fiona Cutting.* Price group A (each clock).

Promotional photograph illustrating a range of Withersdale tile clocks in Art Deco style. 6" tiles. 1983. *Courtesy of Fiona Cutting.* Price group A (each clock).

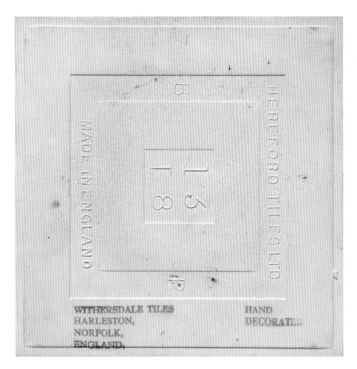

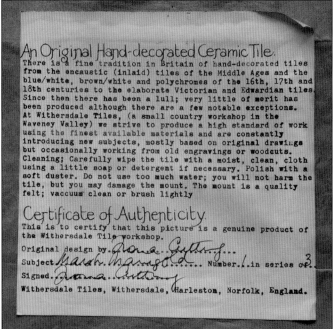

Paper label, "Certificate of Authenticity" signed by Fiona Cutting. 1960s.

Rubber stamp mark on Hereford Tiles 4¼" square blank. Early 1960s.

Rubber stamp mark on Hereford Tiles 4¼" square blank. Late 1960s/early 1970s.

Susan & Douglas Dalgleish
Edinburgh Ceramics 1984-

1984-1988: Adam Pottery, Henderson Row, Stockbridge, Edinburgh, Scotland
1988- : 46 Balcarres Street, Morningside, Edinburgh, Scotland

Susan and Douglas Dalgleish met at Edinburgh College of Art where they both gained BA (Hons) in Art & Design (Ceramics) in 1980. Susan obtained a postgraduate diploma from the same college in 1981 and studied pottery at evening classes whilst Douglas did a postgraduate diploma in ceramics at the same college in 1980-81. On this course, he discovered the British Museum's collection of medieval tiles and attempted to develop a method of encaustic tile production, although this ultimately proved impractical.

In 1981, Susan and Douglas set up a small studio at the Adam Pottery, Henderson Row, Edinburgh, where they researched and developed their tube-line technique. Their first major contract was for three hand painted panels for the Food Hall, Waverley Market Shopping Centre, Edinburgh in 1985; since then, they have successfully completed a large number of commissions for tile panels. They have also undertaken the reproduction and restoration of original Victorian and Edwardian tiles for properties in the city.

Susan and Douglas design and decorate all their own tiles with occasional help on large projects from Susan's son Matthew Finch. They manufacture a wide range of designs, including on-glaze and under-glaze hand painted tiles, and use commercially produced blanks as well as their own hand-made biscuit. They also produce slip-cast, press-molded, tube-lined, and screen printed tiles and mosaics. In 2005, they introduced a range of designs using digitally produced ceramic transfers.

Edinburgh Ceramics have a standard range of leaf and Art Nouveau designs, plus a series of animal tile pictures, many with a distinctive checkered border. In 1995, they produced a new range of pictorial tile panels designed for the Original Tile Company, Edinburgh, which was exhibited at the Period Homes Show, Olympia, London.

Up until 2000, Susan and Douglas used *H. & R. Johnson Ltd.* biscuit tiles for tube-lining and under-glaze work and Johnson's glazed tiles for on-glaze decoration. When Johnson's changed to single fired tiles, however, they had to source biscuit elsewhere and experimented with a number of other manufacturers. They are currently using tiles from B.C.T. (formerly *Candy Tiles Ltd.*) for their hand painted projects and *Clayworth Pottery* for a handmade alternative. They apply water mixable on-glaze and under-glaze colors directly onto the tiles using brushes and sponges. A bulb and nozzle is used for tube-lining and glazes are applied using a spray gun to ensure even application. Most tiles are fired to 1085°C, with on-glaze and luster decoration being fired to 760°C.

Panel of six tube-lined and hand painted tiles depicting a hedgehog family in a checkered border. Each tile 6" square. c.1990. H. & R. Johnson blanks. *Courtesy of and photograph by Edinburgh Ceramics.* Price group C (panel).

Panel of four tube-lined and hand painted tiles depicting a red squirrel in a checkered border. Each tile 6" square. c.1990. H. & R. Johnson blanks. *Courtesy of and photograph by Edinburgh Ceramics.* Price group C (panel).

Panel of four tube-lined and hand painted tiles depicting deer in a checkered border. Each tile 6" square. c.1990. H. & R. Johnson blanks. *Courtesy of and photograph by Edinburgh Ceramics.* Price group C (panel).

Panel of nine tube-lined and hand painted tiles depicting a duck and ducklings in a checkered border. Each tile 6" square. c.1990. H. & R. Johnson blanks. *Courtesy of and photograph by Edinburgh Ceramics.* Price group D (panel).

Panel of six tube-lined and hand painted tiles depicting barnacle geese in a checkered border. Each tile 6" square. c.1990. H. & R. Johnson blanks. *Courtesy of and photograph by Edinburgh Ceramics.* Price group C (panel).

Panel of nine tube-lined and hand painted tiles depicting an Ayrshire cow and calf in a checkered border. Each tile 6" square. c.1990. H. & R. Johnson blanks. *Courtesy of and photograph by Edinburgh Ceramics.* Price group D (panel).

Panel of four tube-lined and hand painted tiles depicting puffins on Bass Rock in a checkered border. Each tile 6" square. c.1990. H. & R. Johnson blanks. *Courtesy of and photograph by Edinburgh Ceramics.* Price group C (panel).

Panel of four tube-lined and hand painted tiles depicting a Frisian cow in a checkered border. Each tile 6" square. c.1990. H. & R. Johnson blanks. *Courtesy of and photograph by Edinburgh Ceramics.* Price group C (panel).

Panel of four tube-lined and hand painted tiles depicting a Blackface Curlyhorn sheep in a checkered border. Each tile 6" square. c.1990. H. & R. Johnson blanks. *Courtesy of and photograph by Edinburgh Ceramics.* Price group C (panel).

Panel of four tube-lined and hand painted tiles depicting a Blackface Grey Leg sheep in a checkered border. Each tile 6" square. c.1990. H. & R. Johnson blanks. *Courtesy of and photograph by Edinburgh Ceramics.* Price group C (panel).

Panel of nine tube-lined and hand painted tiles depicting an elephant with young in an elephant skin border. Each tile 6" square. c.1990. H. & R. Johnson blanks. *Courtesy of and photograph by Edinburgh Ceramics.* Price group D (panel).

Panel of four tube-lined and hand painted tiles depicting a Gloucester Old Spot pig in a checkered border. Each tile 6" square. c.1990. H. & R. Johnson blanks. *Courtesy of and photograph by Edinburgh Ceramics.* Price group C (panel).

Panel of twelve tube-lined and hand painted tiles depicting a safari scene in a giraffe skin border. Each tile 6" square. c.1990. H. & R. Johnson blanks. *Courtesy of and photograph by Edinburgh Ceramics.* Price group D (panel).

Panel of tube-lined and hand painted tiles depicting the Garden of Eden, "I just happen to like apples and I'm not afraid of snakes. Ani di Franco," in a border of relief molded and hand painted tiles. Each full tile 6" square. c.1990. *Courtesy of and photograph by Edinburgh Ceramics.* Price group E (panel).

Tube-lined and hand painted tile depicting a crab and panel of two tiles depicting a lobster, both in checkered frames. Each tile 6" square. c.1990. H. & R. Johnson blanks. *Courtesy of and photograph by Edinburgh Ceramics.* Price group B.

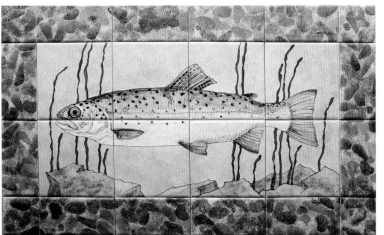

Panel of eight tube-lined and hand painted tiles depicting a trout set in a frame of pebble pattern tiles. Each full tile 6" square. c.1990. H. & R. Johnson blanks. *Courtesy of and photograph by Edinburgh Ceramics.* Price group D (panel).

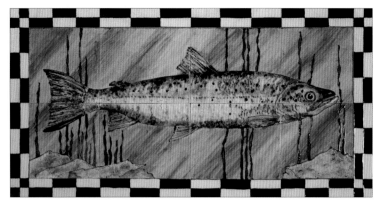

Panel of eight tube-lined and hand painted tiles depicting a salmon in a checkered border. Each tile 6" square. c.1990. H. & R. Johnson blanks. *Courtesy of and photograph by Edinburgh Ceramics*. Price group D (panel).

Tube-lined and hand painted tile depicting a harvest mouse in a checkered border. 6" square. c.1990. H. & R. Johnson blank. *Courtesy of and photograph by Edinburgh Ceramics*. Price group B.

Tube-lined and hand painted tile depicting the frog prince in a checkered border. 6" square. 1993. H. & R. Johnson blank. Price group B.

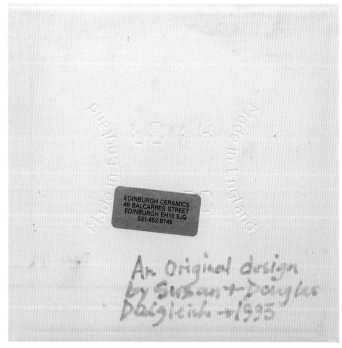

Back of tube-lined and hand painted tile depicting the frog prince in a checkered border. 6" square. 1993. H. & R. Johnson blank.

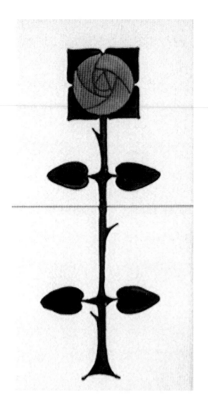

Panel of two tube-lined tiles depicting an Art Nouveau rose in the style of Charles Rennie Mackintosh. Each tile 6" square. c.1998. H. & R. Johnson blanks. *Courtesy of and photograph by Edinburgh Ceramics.* Price group B (panel).

Hand painted over-glaze tile depicting "The Tile Collector," designed and painted by Susan Dalgleish. 6" square. September 1993. This tile was specially painted by Susan for the author after they had attended a Tiles & Architectural Ceramics Society outing to Marlborough, Wiltshire in 1993. Price group C.

Identification and Marks

Tile panels are signed "Susan + Douglas Dalgleish," often with the appropriate year.

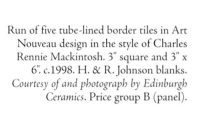

Run of five tube-lined border tiles in Art Nouveau design in the style of Charles Rennie Mackintosh. 3" square and 3" x 6". c.1998. H. & R. Johnson blanks. *Courtesy of and photograph by Edinburgh Ceramics.* Price group B (panel).

Self-adhesive label and signature. This label has been in use since 1984.

Panel of nine hand painted tiles depicting male and female pheasants. Each tile 6" square. c.1998. H. & R. Johnson blanks. *Courtesy of and photograph by Edinburgh Ceramics.* Price group C (panel).

Majel Davidson (1885-1969) 1920s and 1930s

Aberdeen, Scotland and Powis House, Near Stirling, Scotland

Majel Davidson was born in Aberdeen and graduated from Gray's School of Art in 1907. Between 1908 and 1909, she studied under Guerin in Paris, where she was influenced by the Colourists. Sometime during the 1920s, she lived in Toronto and was involved with a group of artists who were known as The Group of Seven. It is likely that she became interested in ceramics at this time and a kiln was built for her near Aberdeen. She settled at Powis House, near Stirling, with other women artists who became known as the Powis Group.

Her tiles are all in very strong Art Deco style featuring dancers, birds, fish, and stylized plants. The technique appears to be tin-glaze using in-glaze colors. Known examples of her work have been found on *J. H. Barratt* and *H. & R. Johnson Ltd.* blanks. She also used *J. C. Edwards* "Adamantine" dust-pressed floor tiles when a red body was required.

Hand painted tile depicting a dancer. 6" square. c.1930. H. & R. Johnson blank. *Courtesy of Michael Spender.* Price group C.

Hand painted tile depicting a dancer. 6" square. c.1930. H. & R. Johnson blank. *Courtesy of Michael Spender.* Price group C.

Panel of six hand painted tiles depicting dancers and scenery. Each tile 6" square. c.1930. J. H. Barratt blanks. *Courtesy of Brenda Sultan, photograph by Jonathan Sultan.* Price group E (panel).

Hand painted tile depicting fish. 6" square. c.1930. J. H. Barratt blank. *Courtesy of Brenda Sultan, photograph by Jonathan Sultan.* Price group C.

Hand painted tile depicting a frog. 6" square. c.1930. J. H. Barratt blank. *Courtesy of Brenda Sultan, photograph by Jonathan Sultan.* Price group C.

Derek Davis 1955-1994

1952-1955: Hillesden Community, Buckinghamshire.
1955-1994: Duff House, 13 Maltravers Street, Arundel, West Sussex

Derek Maynard Davis was one of the co-founders of the Hillesden Community in Buckinghamshire, where he met and worked alongside *Eric Mellon*. In 1955, he moved to Arundel and established his own small pottery working mainly to commission, creating hand painted, molded, and relief tiles in oxidized and reduced stonewares.

In 1963, he completed a large tile panel for the Ford Motor Co. at Brentwood, Essex and in 1966, he exhibited at Liberty's in London and Macy's in New York. He ceased potting in 1994 and now concentrates on painting in oils.

Hand built stoneware tile with an abstract design. 10" square in original frame. 1980s. *Courtesy of Derek Maynard Davis.* Price group D.

Hand painted tile depicting a duck in flight. 6" square. c.1930. J. H. Barratt blank. *Courtesy of Brenda Sultan, photograph by Jonathan Sultan.* Price group C.

Identification and Marks
No identifying marks.

Hand built stoneware tile with an abstract design. 10" square in original frame. 1980s. *Courtesy of Derek Maynard Davis.* Price group D.

Hand built stoneware tile with an abstract design. 10" x 16" in original frame. 1980s. *Courtesy of Derek Maynard Davis.* Price group D.

Panel of eight stoneware tiles with applied decoration. Each tile 8" square in original frame. 1980s. *Courtesy of Derek Maynard Davis.* Price group E (panel).

Hand built stoneware tile with an abstract design. 10" x 14" in original frame. 1980s. *Courtesy of Derek Maynard Davis.* Price group D.

Hand built stoneware tile with an abstract design. 6" square in original frame. 1980s. *Courtesy of Derek Maynard Davis.* Price group C.

Composite tiled floor consisting of individually shaped tiles representing leaves etc. 1970s. *Courtesy of and photograph by Derek Maynard Davis.*

Hand built stoneware tile with an abstract design. 18" square in original frame. 1980s. *Courtesy of Derek Maynard Davis.* Price group D.

Four shaped stoneware tiles in the form of leaves and a snail. 1970s. *Courtesy of Derek Maynard Davis.* Price group B (each element).

Identification and Marks
No identifying marks.

Josse Davis 1981-

84 Maltravers Street, Arundel, West Sussex

Born in 1959, Josse is the son of ceramic artist and painter *Derek Davis* and painter Ruth Davis. Following a foundation course at the West Sussex College of Art and Design from 1977-78, he went on to take a degree in ceramics at the Bath Academy of Art. He has held a number of posts as teacher and lecturer in ceramics at various Sussex and Hampshire colleges.

Josse recalls, "As a child, I was surrounded by pottery and painting. My father introduced me to the wheel and throwing when I was three and I remember him having to restrain me from dismantling the brick kiln door before it was cool enough to open. Only then was I allowed to crawl inside and pass out the pots and I can still close my eyes and see those glazes. I was hooked."

A confident draughtsman, Josse draws most of his inspiration from the world of nature. His approach to decoration is traditionally English and his work can be divided into two distinct styles: the spontaneous and the disciplined. His tiles are decorated under-glaze using natural oxides fired to 1080°C (cone 03). Prior to 1985, he decorated on his own handmade terra-cotta blanks but since that time he has used blanks from *H. & R. Johnson Ltd.*.

Panel of forty-two hand painted tiles depicting tigers. Each tile 6" square in original frame. c.1985. H. & R. Johnson blanks. *Courtesy of Josse Davis.* Price group F (panel).

Hand painted tile depicting tigers in the undergrowth. 6" square. 1980s. H. & R. Johnson blanks. *Courtesy of Josse Davis.* Price group B.

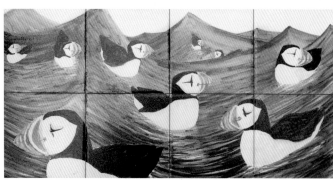

Panel of six hand painted tiles depicting a tiger. Each tile 6" square. 1980s. H. & R. Johnson blanks. *Courtesy of Josse Davis*. Price group D (panel).

Panel of eight hand painted tiles depicting puffins. Each tile 6" square. 1990s. H. & R. Johnson blanks. *Courtesy of Josse Davis*. Price group D (panel).

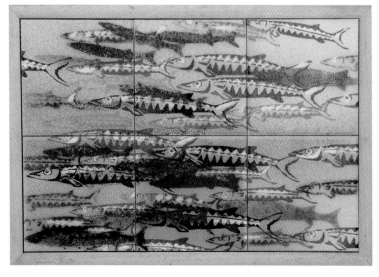

Panel of eighteen hand painted tiles depicting a jungle scene. Each tile 6" square. 1990s. H. & R. Johnson blanks. *Courtesy of Josse Davis*. Price group E (panel).

Panel of six hand painted tiles depicting barracudas. Each tile 6" square in original frame. 1980s. H. & R. Johnson blanks. *Courtesy of Josse Davis*. Price group D (panel).

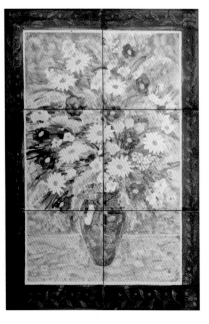

Panel of six hand painted tiles depicting a vase of flowers. Each tile 6" square. 1990s. H. & R. Johnson blanks. *Courtesy of Josse Davis*. Price group D (panel).

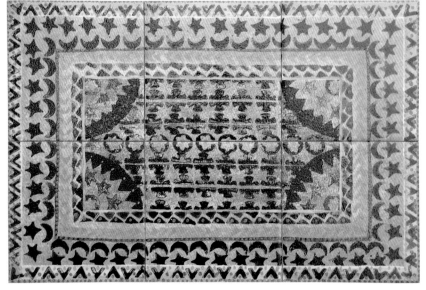

Panel of six hand painted tiles depicting an oriental rug. Each tile 6" square. 1990s. H. & R. Johnson blanks. *Courtesy of Josse Davis*. Price group D (panel).

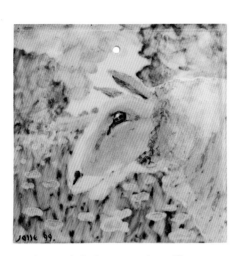

Hand painted tile depicting a sheep. 6" square. 1999. H. & R. Johnson blank. *Courtesy of Josse Davis.* Price group B.

Hand painted tile depicting a sheep. 6" square. 1999. H. & R. Johnson blank. *Courtesy of Josse Davis.* Price group B.

Hand painted tile depicting two sheep. 6" square. 1999. H. & R. Johnson blank. *Courtesy of Josse Davis.* Price group B.

Panel of nine hand painted tiles depicting Noah's Ark. Each tile 6" square. 1990s. H. & R. Johnson blanks. *Courtesy of Josse Davis.* Price group D (panel).

Identification and Marks

JOSSE

Painted signature used on front of tiles, often with year (e.g., 99 for 1999).

C. James Dring (b.1905-d.1985) 1932-1947   Identification and Marks

South London (probably Clapham)

C. James Dring studied Art at Clapham in South London during the mid to late 1920s and went on to study under William Rothenstein at the Royal College of Art, graduating in 1931. Here he met and was influenced by *William Staite Murray*, who taught him ceramics. He mainly painted in oils and watercolor but also produced a few hand painted tiles and dishes between 1932 and 1947. His tiles appear to have been decorated on biscuit bought in from *Carter & Co.* or *Poole Pottery*, and it is possible they were fired at Poole or in Staite Murray's own kiln.

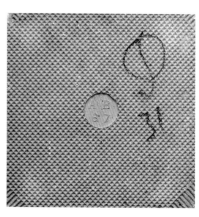

Painted mark on Carter & Co. 6" square blank. The painted number "31" indicates this tile was decorated in 1931.

Hand painted tile with a floral design. 6" square. 1931. Carter & Co. blank. Price group B.

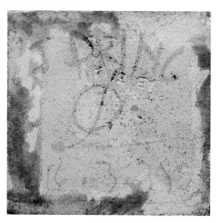

Painted marks on Carter & Co. 5" square plastic clay blank. This tile is dated in full on the bottom "14.3.35"(?).

Hand painted tile depicting a rabbit. 5" square. 1935. Carter & Co. blank. Price group B.

Heather & Michel Ducos
Alford Pottery 1993-

Commercial Road, Alford, Lincolnshire

Alford Pottery was established by Heather & Michel Ducos in 1972, producing a large range of stoneware pottery, hand-thrown on the premises. Products included tableware, kitchenware, and some giftware. In the early 1990s, they started to produce hand-made stoneware tiles designed by Michel Ducos. More recently, they have concentrated on hand painting commercial bisque tile purchased from *H. & R. Johnson Ltd.* and *H. & E. Smith Ltd.*. They specialize in in-glaze painted panels and tile tables using their own glazes and colors. These are mainly produced to commission and are particularly popular for use in kitchens.

Panel of twelve hand painted tiles depicting a bowl of fruit. Each tile 4" square. 1990s. Unknown commercial blanks. *Courtesy of and photograph by Heather & Michel Ducos.* Price group C (panel).

Panel of nine hand painted tiles depicting a cockerel. Each tile 4" square. 1990s. Unknown commercial blanks. *Courtesy of and photograph by Heather & Michel Ducos.* Price group C (panel).

Identification and Marks
No identifying marks.

Joan Duffus 1930s

Joan Duffus appears to have been a talented artist who created a number of decorated tiles during the 1930s on commercial and handmade plastic clay blanks.

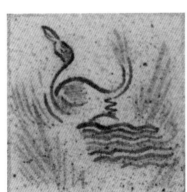

Hand painted tile depicting a duck. 4" square. c.1930. Unknown commercial blank. *Courtesy of Carolyn Wraight.* Price group B.

Hand painted plastic clay tile depicting a deer. 5" square. c.1930. *Courtesy of Carolyn Wraight.* Price group B.

Identification and Marks

Left: plastic clay tile. 5" square with incised signature. Right: commercial blank. 4" square. Cork backed with handwritten signature.

Angela Evans 1992-

1992-1998: Hoxton Square, London
1998- : Unit 3, Level 5 (north), New England House, New England Street, Brighton, East Sussex.

Angela Evans has been making tiles since 1992. In 1997, her husband Richard Wells joined her, just before they relocated from London to Brighton. Angela's early designs feature bold non-figurative patterns in rich colors, often created using found objects to impress designs into the clay. Her more recent designs feature fruit and vegetables, the molds for which are created by freezing actual produce. The tiles are press-molded and extruded and are fired at 1060°C in an oxidizing atmosphere. Glazes are all hand painted. A recent development is the manufacture of "pseudo-mosaic" tiles that are used to frame mirrors.

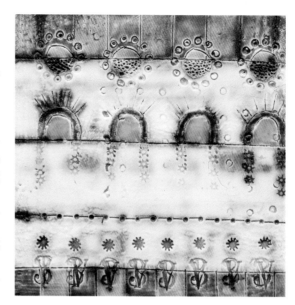

Impressed, incised, and hand painted plastic clay tile with an abstract design. 6" square. Early 1990s. *Courtesy of Angela Evans.* Price group B.

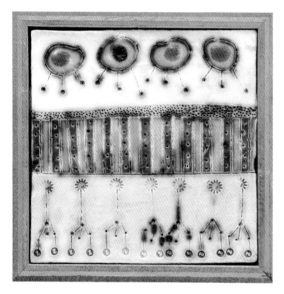

Impressed, incised, and hand painted plastic clay tile with an abstract design. 6" square in original frame. Early 1990s. *Courtesy of Angela Evans.* Price group B.

Hand modeled and part glazed plastic clay tile with an abstract design. 6" square. Early 1990s. *Courtesy of Angela Evans.* Price group B.

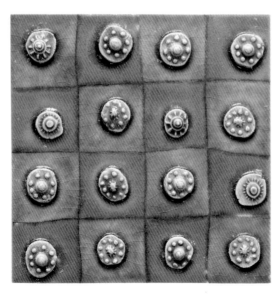

Sprigged and hand painted plastic clay tile with an abstract design. 6" square. Early 1990s. *Courtesy of Angela Evans.* Price group B.

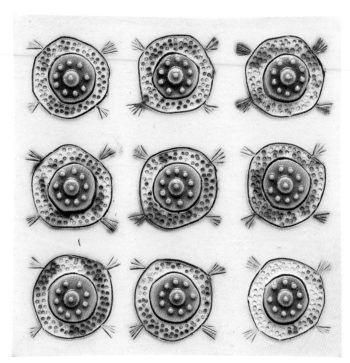

Sprigged, incised, and hand painted plastic clay tile with an abstract design. 6" square. Early 1990s. *Courtesy of Angela Evans.* Price group B.

Impressed, incised, modeled, and hand painted plastic clay tile toothbrush holder with an abstract design. Approx. 9" x 4½". Early 1990s. *Courtesy of Angela Evans.* Price group B.

Sprigged, impressed, and glazed plastic clay tile with a heart design. 6" square. Early 1990s. *Courtesy of Angela Evans.* Price group B.

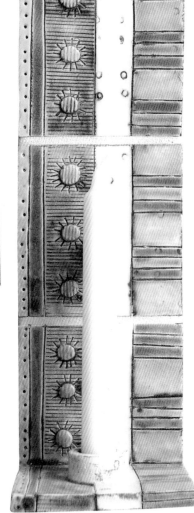

Impressed, incised, and hand painted plastic clay tile candle sconce with an abstract design. Each tile 4" square. Early 1990s. *Courtesy of Angela Evans.* Price group B.

Twelve miniature plastic clay tiles in various techniques. Each tile approx. 2" square. Mid-1990s. *Courtesy of Angela Evans*. Price group A (each tile).

Impressed, incised, and hand painted plastic clay tile shelf with a flower design. Each tile approx. 5" square. Early 1990s. *Courtesy of Angela Evans*. Price group B.

Twelve miniature plastic clay tiles in various techniques. Each tile approx. 2" square. Mid-1990s. *Courtesy of Angela Evans*. Price group A (each tile).

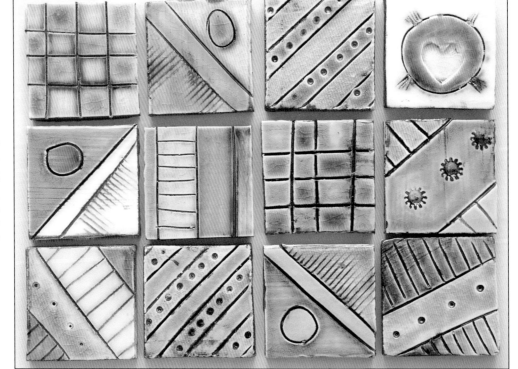

High relief molded plastic clay tile with a floral design. 4" square. Mid-1990s. *Courtesy of Angela Evans.* Price group A.

Four high relief molded plastic clay tiles with fruit designs. Each tile 4" square. Late-1990s. *Courtesy of Angela Evans.* Price group A (each).

Two panels of two high relief molded plastic clay tiles depicting sweet corn and peppers. Each tile 4" square. Late-1990s. *Courtesy of Angela Evans.* Price group A (each panel).

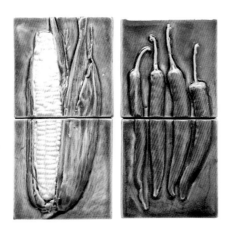

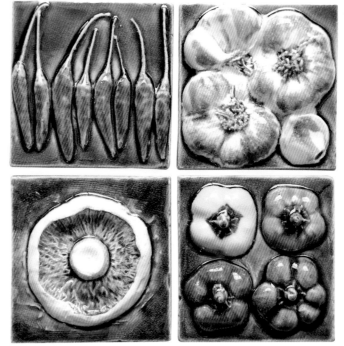

Four high relief molded plastic clay tiles with vegetable designs. Each tile 4" square. Late-1990s. *Courtesy of Angela Evans.* Price group A (each).

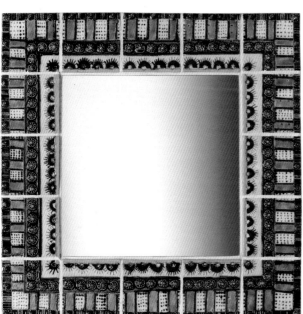

Mirror with sixteen relief molded, impressed, and incised tiles forming a frame, "Firework" design. Each tile 4" square. Mid-1990s. *Courtesy of and photograph by Angela Evans.* Price group C (mirror complete).

Identification and Marks
    No identifying marks.

Frank Fidler (b.1910-d.1995)

1954-1963: London
1963-1995: 130 High Street, Barkway, Royston, Hertfordshire

Frank Fidler was the son of a rose grower who decided whilst still at school that he wanted to become an artist. It was not until he was thirty-seven, however, that he started to paint; even then, he continued to run a greengrocer's shop in Waltham Cross until 1954. That year, he sold his business and became a full-time artist. He was initially influenced by Abstract Expressionism and action painting, and exhibited in Moscow in 1957 and Paris in 1959. Later in his life, he abandoned abstraction and began to record the landscape around his home in pastels, watercolor, and pencil. He continued to draw until his death in 1995.

In the early 1960s, Frank developed an interest in ceramics and designed and decorated tiles that he sold through the Design Centre in London. His earlier tiles were painted in rich glazes over pre-glazed commercial tiles. For some of his later work, he employed an unusual and possibly unique technique. This involved applying a layer of liquid glaze to a commercial glazed tile and then overlaying this with a thin film of clay that was allowed to dry, creating a surface criss-crossed with small fissures or cracks. This was then impressed with various objects, including small cogwheels and tubes. In addition, some of the clay was occasionally wiped away with a finger and a further layer of contrasting colored glaze inserted. On some tiles, a further translucent glaze was applied over the whole surface. Firing then took place in an electric kiln.

Frank used commercial tiles purchased from *Richards Tiles Ltd.* (c.1963), *Pilkington's Tiles Ltd.* (late 1960s), and *H. & R. Johnson Ltd.* (early 1970s). He had a standard range of tile designs and a brochure issued c.1970 illustrated twenty designs, of which twelve are shown as being selected for display at the Design Centre in London. In addition to individual tiles, Frank also undertook commissions, including two ceramic murals for the Civic Centre in St. Albans, Hertfordshire.

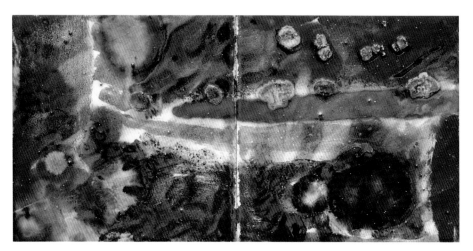

Panel of two hand painted tiles with an abstract design. Each tile 6" square. 1963. Richards Tiles blanks. Price group D (panel).

Impressed, incised, and hand painted tile with an abstract design. 6" square. 1973. H. & R. Johnson blank. The decoration on this tile has been achieved by covering a pre-fired biscuit tile with an engobe, into which various objects have been impressed. The tile was then left to dry, causing shrinkage of the engobe, then painted with glaze over the top. Price group C.

Hand painted tile with an abstract design. 6" square. 1963. Richards Tiles blank. *Courtesy of Adrian Grater.* Price group B.

Impressed, incised, and hand painted tile with an abstract design. 6" square. 1976. Pilkington's Tiles blank. The decoration on this tile has been achieved by covering a pre-fired biscuit tile with an engobe, into which various objects have been impressed. The tile was then left to dry, causing shrinkage of the engobe, then painted with glaze over the top. Price group C.

Identification and Marks
No identifying marks.

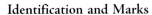

Hand painted plastic clay tile with a floral design. 4" square. 1993. Price group A.

Andrew Fisher
Andrew Fisher Ceramic Design 1991-c.2000

17 Vincent Road, Sheffield.

Andrew Fisher trained in ceramics at Middlesex Polytechnic from 1981-85, and in 1991 established Andrew Fisher Ceramic Design with his wife Naomi. His early tiles were slip decorated, and it took considerable experimentation over a number of months to overcome various production problems. The couple then moved on to produce tin-glazed tiles that have proved to be much more successful.

In addition to large tile panels, Andrew and Naomi produced a range of standard maiolica picture tiles, many of which featured seaside objects such as fish, shells, and crabs, predominantly in blue with splashes of yellow. Other patterns were based on floral designs and stylized leaf patterns. The tiles were produced on a red-firing earthenware body produced in-house. The back of the tiles has a distinctive texture resulting from the use of a fine cloth on which the clay was rolled. The standard production size was 4" square.

Hand painted plastic clay tile depicting a crab. 4" square. 1993. Price group A.

Hand painted plastic clay tile depicting a fish. 4" square. 1993. Price group A.

Detail of hand painted plastic clay tile panel depicting a pheasant. Each tile 4" square. c.1993. *Courtesy of and photograph by Andrew Fisher.* Price group C (panel).

Detail of hand painted plastic clay tile panel depicting lemons and grapes. Each tile 4" square. c.1993. *Courtesy of and photograph by Andrew Fisher.* Price group C (panel).

Identification and Marks

Self-adhesive label. 1991-c.2000

References
Maiolica Picture Tiles and *Blue and White Maiolica Tiles,* two leaflets produced by the company c.1993.

Claude Frere-Smith 1976-

75 Margrove Park, Boosbeck, Saltburn-by-Sea, North Yorkshire

Claude Frere-Smith has been making handmade and hand decorated tiles since 1976, utilizing high-fired stoneware and porcelain and low-fired earthenware with raku glazes. He has also used porcelain paper clay, raw glazed and once-fired to 1250°C. He employs a variety of decorative techniques, including free-hand modeling, drawing, and sgraffito.

Porcelain paper clay tile with under-glaze color and sgraffito drawing depicting "Margrove Park." Approx. 6" across. c.2000. *Courtesy of and photograph by Claude Frere-Smith.* Price group B.

Porcelain paper clay tile with hand modeling and under-glaze color depicting "Slapwath." Approx. 6" across. c.2000. *Courtesy of and photograph by Claude Frere-Smith.* Price group B.

Identification and Marks

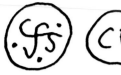

Variety of painted marks used by Claude Frere-Smith. 1976-

Alan Frewin
Millhouse Pottery 1980-

1 Station Road, Harleston, Norfolk

Alan Frewin established Millhouse Pottery about 1980, and creates beautiful handmade tiles—which he prefers to call plaques or ceramic paintings—using colored slips on his own earthenware blanks. His inspiration is taken from the work of artists such as Gustav Klimt or historic associations and sometimes, heraldic devices.

Barbotine painted plastic clay tile depicting a female portrait in the style of Klimt. Approx. 10" x 8" in original frame. c.1999. *Courtesy of and photograph by Alan Frewin.* Price group B.

Barbotine painted plastic clay plaque depicting a hen. Approx. 8" x 6". c.1999. *Courtesy of and photograph by Alan Frewin.* Price group B.

Barbotine painted plastic clay tile depicting a king and queen. Approx. 10" x 8". c.1999. *Courtesy of and photograph by Alan Frewin.* Price group B.

Identification and Marks

Painted mark used on the back of tiles. 1980 on.

Elspeth Gardner
Elspeth Gardner Ceramics 1991-

Strathclyde Business Centre, Carstairs Street, Glasgow, Scotland

Elspeth Gardner's interest in tiles began while she was a student at Glasgow School of Art. The chosen subject for her dissertation was "Glasgow's Housing Since 1945." In the course of researching this, she became interested in the mass destruction of many of the older tenement buildings, butchers, fishmongers, and dairies (so typical of late 19th and early 20th century Glasgow), nearly all of which were decorated with tiles.

As a ceramics student, she began to focus on these tiles and completed her studies at Staffordshire University in Stoke-on-Trent, attaining her MA. There she learnt the technique of tube-lining, which she subsequently used for most of her tile designs. Returning to Glasgow in 1991, Elspeth established a studio and began production, supplying shops throughout the U.K. and beyond. She also makes tiles and tile panels to commission. Her specialty is still tube-lining, but over the years she has extended her techniques to include slip painting, on-glaze decoration, hand glazing, color matching, and tile reproduction.

Panel of four tube-lined and hand painted tiles depicting "Hermit the Crab." Each tile 6" square surrounded by ½" wide border tiles. c.1999. H. & R. Johnson blanks. *Courtesy of Elspeth Gardner.* Price group C (panel).

Panel of sixteen tube-lined and hand painted tiles depicting "Hens." Each tile 100mm square. c.1999. Clayworth Pottery blanks. *Courtesy of Elspeth Gardner.* Price group D (panel).

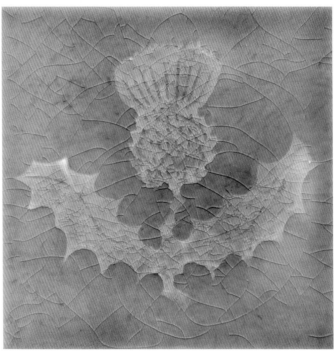

Slip painted tile depicting a thistle. 150mm square. c.1999. H. & R. Johnson blank. Price group A.

Tube-lined tile depicting a lighthouse scene. 150mm square. c.1999. H. & R. Johnson blank. Price group A.

Tube-lined tile depicting puffins. 150mm square. c.1999. H. & R. Johnson blank. Price group A.

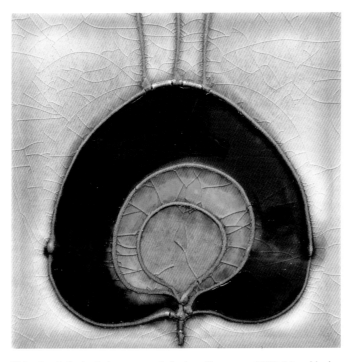

Tube-lined tile depicting a peacock feather. 6" square. c.1999. Mosa blank (Netherlands). Price group A.

Identification and Marks

Individual tiles are unmarked but tile panels are signed with her initials or full name.

Maria Geurten (b.1929-d.1998) 1966-1998

1966-1984: Penzance, Cornwall
1984-1998: Elm Hill, Norwich, Norfolk

Maria Geurten was born in Hergum near Maastricht in the Netherlands. She was educated at Maastricht and Amsterdam and took up painting and ceramics in her twenties. In 1966, she married and moved to England, establishing a small pottery in Penzance, Cornwall. The pottery operated mainly during the summer months and, besides her husband, Keith Smith, there were usually four other potters employed. While at Penzance, Maria occasionally made hand painted tiles on commercial blanks depicting local scenes, but most of her tiles date from her move to Norwich in 1984. There she specialized in handmade stoneware tiles with incised designs, mainly of birds and flowers. The clay was rolled flat on a canvas separating layer and the design was cut into the clay with a drawing needle. After drying for a couple of days, the tiles were fettled and colored using copper, cobalt, manganese, and iron oxides. Firing took place at 1050°C in an electric kiln. Some of the more popular designs were repeated by creating a mold from an original incised tile and then producing copies from the mold. Towards the end of her life, Maria made fewer tiles and concentrated mainly on painting. She died in 1998.

Hand incised stoneware tile with a floral design. 4" square. c.1985. *Courtesy of Zena Corrigan.* Price group B.

Hand incised stoneware tile depicting a dove. 4" square. c.1985. *Courtesy of Zena Corrigan.* Price group B.

Hand painted tile depicting a river scene. 6" square. c.1978. Unknown commercial blank. Taken from a promotional leaflet. Price group B.

Hand incised stoneware tile depicting a woodland scene. 4" square. c.1990. *Courtesy of Roger Hensman.* Price group B.

Hand incised stoneware tile depicting a jug of flowers. 4" square. c.1990. *Courtesy of Roger Hensman.* Price group B.

Self-adhesive label. 1984-1998. *Courtesy of Roger Hensman.*

Joanna Goddard
Joanna Goddard Ceramics 1993-

11 Margaret Street, Brighton, East Sussex

Joanna Goddard was born in Brighton, Sussex in 1969, where she lives and works. Since graduating in 1993, she has exhibited regularly in Britain and Europe. She has also worked to commission for private clients, making tableware and transfer printed tiles. In 1998, she researched a new style of artwork inspired by microbiology, inflatable toys, and the organic style of Japanese architecture. In the studio, her process begins with visual and technical research but the final form of her work is only revealed after many stages of re-drawing and re-modeling.

Joanna's tiles are press-molded from plastic clay and hand painted. She also works with transfer prints that she applies onto her own handmade and occasionally commercial biscuit. The transfer prints are applied in a third firing at 800°C.

Hand incised stoneware tile depicting a pair of doves. 4" square. c.1990. *Courtesy of Roger Hensman.* Price group B.

Identification and Marks
Maria's early hand-painted tiles are signed on the front "M. Geurten."

Detail of biscuit fired paper clay tile impressed with type. Actual size of tile 150mm square. 1998. *Courtesy of and photograph by Joanna Goddard.* Price group B.

Composite panel of transfer printed handmade tiles entitled "Forgotten Species." Overall size 1200mm x 600mm. 1996. *Courtesy of and photograph by Joanna Goddard.* Price group E (panel).

Detail of "Forgotten Species" tile panel. This panel was inspired by seeing pictures of the Russian royal family, which led to research into the isolated existence of royalty at that time. *Courtesy of and photograph by Joanna Goddard.*

Composite panel of transfer printed handmade tiles entitled "His & Hers, His." Overall size approx. 1000mm wide. 1997. *Courtesy of and photograph by Joanna Goddard.* Price group E (panel).

Composite panel of transfer printed handmade tiles entitled "His & Hers, Hers." Overall size approx. 1000mm wide. 1997. *Courtesy of and photograph by Joanna Goddard.* Price group E (panel).

Identification and Marks
No identifying marks.

Joan Godfrey

1958-1961: Chauntry Road, Maidenhead, Berkshire
1962- : The Studio, Kiln Cottage, Boase Street, Newlyn, Cornwall

Joan Godfrey's introduction to clay was at an evening class in clay modeling. From this she developed an interest in making tiles and established her first studio at Maidenhead in Berkshire in 1958. Her early tiles were relief molded and she still works in this technique on occasion today, but most of her tiles are decorated with colored glazes on commercial preglazed tiles. She has also experimented with glass fusion and has combined this technique with colored glazes to produce a range of abstract designs in bold, vivid colors. She uses blanks from *H. & R. Johnson Ltd.*

Nine glass fusion tiles, "Orange Centre." Each tile 6" square. 1980s. H. & R. Johnson blanks. *Courtesy of and photograph by Joan Godfrey.* Price group A (each).

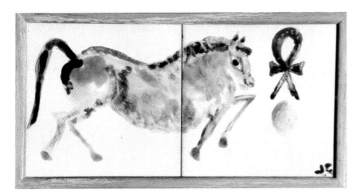

Panel of two hand painted over-glaze tiles, "Egyptian Horse." Each tile 6" square in original frame. 1980s. H. & R. Johnson blanks. *Courtesy of and photograph by Joan Godfrey.* Price group B (panel).

Identification and Marks

Early tiles are stamped on the back "Joan Godfrey"; more recent tiles have her initials "JG" painted on the front.

Paul Gooderham
Gailey Pottery 1980-

1976-1979: Factory Road, Handsworth, Birmingham
1980- : The Old Church, Watling Street, Gailey, Staffordshire

After studying at Wolverhampton University, Paul Gooderham established his first studio in part of an old brass foundry in Handsworth, Birmingham in 1976. This was sponsored by a Birmingham businessman who had seen Paul's degree show and believed that his work could be commercially successful. By 1979, the premises had become too small and Paul relocated to a disused church at Gailey in Staffordshire, which provided him with ideal new premises.

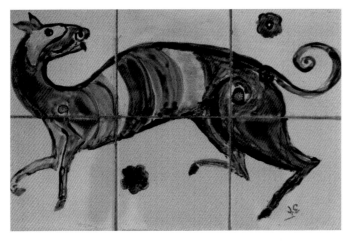

Detail of panel hand painted over-glaze tiles, "Kell's Beast." Each tile 6" square. 1980s. H. & R. Johnson blanks. *Courtesy of and photograph by Joan Godfrey.* Price group C (panel).

Shaped and impressed stoneware tile inspired by a 1930s radio design. Size unknown. c.1974. *Courtesy of and photograph by Paul Gooderham.* Price group C.

In the new studio, he soon employed a staff of two helping him to make his pots, plaques, and tiles in stoneware and porcelain. He uses an unusual technique of inlaying porcelain into stoneware and stoneware into porcelain. The resultant tiles and pots are glazed with homemade ash glazes and Paul specializes in overlap glazing, creating wonderful soft effects. His designs are chiefly landscapes and are uniquely his in style. Most of his tiles are one-offs and he has also completed a number of public commissions. He has also worked as artist-in-residence in a number of schools.

Incised and hand painted stoneware tile depicting daisies. Size unknown. 1990s. *Courtesy of and photograph by Paul Gooderham.* Price group C.

Shaped and impressed stoneware tile inspired by a 1930s radio design. Size unknown. c.1974. *Courtesy of and photograph by Paul Gooderham.* Price group C.

Incised and hand painted stoneware tile depicting a copse. 8" x 3½". 1980s. *Courtesy of Peter & Diana Clegg.* Price group C.

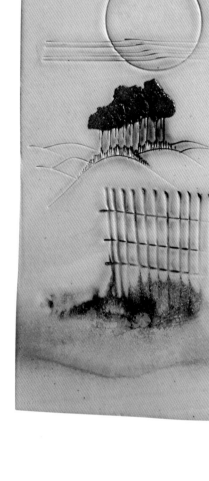

Incised, hand built, and hand painted stoneware tile depicting a window scene. Size unknown. 1990s. *Courtesy of and photograph by Paul Gooderham.* Price group C.

Incised and hand painted stoneware tile depicting a landscape. Size unknown. 1990s. *Courtesy of and photograph by Paul Gooderham*. Price group C.

Incised and hand painted stoneware tile depicting a landscape. 6″ diameter. 1980s. *Courtesy of Peter & Diana Clegg*. Price group C.

Incised and hand painted stoneware tile depicting a landscape. Size unknown. 1990s. *Courtesy of and photograph by Paul Gooderham*. Price group C.

Self-adhesive label. 1976-

Incised and hand painted stoneware tile depicting a landscape. Size unknown. 1990s. *Courtesy of and photograph by Paul Gooderham.* Price group C.

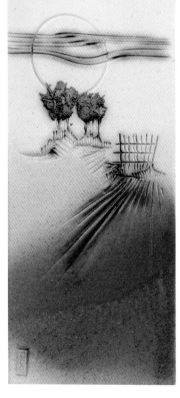

Incised and hand painted stoneware tile depicting a landscape. 8" x 3½". 1990s. *Courtesy of and photograph by Paul Gooderham.* Price group C.

Carol Ann Greenway
Classical Ceramics (formerly Greenway Associates) 1996-

33 Downside, Ventnor, Isle of Wight

Carol Ann Greenway studied at Central St. Martin's College of Art & Design in London for six years, obtaining a BA (Hons) in Ceramic Design and subsequently a Masters in Industrial Design. She specialized in tiles and particularly in those of the Victorian era. As she has lived in the Middle East, Fiji, Japan, and Papua New Guinea, the culture of these countries is reflected in her work, but she is equally at home working with designs based on fruits and flowers of the British Isles. Following work experience with *Kenneth Clark Ceramics*, she established her own business in 1996.

Incised and hand painted stoneware tile depicting a landscape. Size unknown. 1990s. *Courtesy of and photograph by Paul Gooderham.* Price group C.

Relief molded, partly glazed experimental tile with a geometric design. 6" square. 1990s. Made on Carol Greenway's own small dust-press. *Courtesy of Carol Ann Greenway.* Price group A.

Her earliest tiles were dust-pressed in her own studio and fired in a small electric kiln. The designs were simple geometric patterns, glazed or partly glazed. Although she still makes slip-cast tiles using plaster molds that she sculpts herself, most of her production is now tube-lined on *H. & R. Johnson Ltd.* commercial blanks. She makes her own glazes and specializes in large scale, specially commissioned murals, but also produces a range of smaller panels for tabletops etc.

Hand screen printed commemorative tile, "Ventura Pekingese Club, 1947-1997. 6" square. 1997. H. & R. Johnson blank. *Courtesy of Carol Ann Greenway.* Price group A.

Sponge mottled experimental tile. 6" square. 1990s. Made on Carol Greenway's own small dust-press. *Courtesy of Carol Ann Greenway.* Price group A.

Panel of tube-lined tiles depicting insects. Each tile 6" square. 1990s. H. & R. Johnson blanks. *Courtesy of Carol Ann Greenway.* Price group A (each tile).

Detail of tube-lined kitchen tile panel depicting an apple bough. Each tile 6" square. 1990s. *Courtesy of Carol Ann Greenway.* Price group C (panel).

Panel of forty-eight tube-lined tiles depicting irises, butterflies, and moths. Each tile 6" square. 1990s. H. & R. Johnson blanks. Photographed in the artist's studio. *Courtesy of Carol Ann Greenway.* Price group F (panel).

Identification and Marks

Painted mark. 1996-

Eleanor created many of her screens herself using indirect stencils but also had some of her designs made up for her by Sericol, a commercial ceramics screen print manufacturer. The designs were printed onto pre-glazed white tiles made by *H. & R. Johnson Ltd.* and were fired at biscuit temperature of 1040°C to achieve an in-glaze result. Seventeen of her standard designs were selected by the Design Council for display in their London and Glasgow showrooms. Her tiles were also used at Windsor Castle, the Tate Gallery, the Natural History Museum, and the Law Society in London. There are representative collections of her tiles at the Museum of Domestic Design and Architecture at Middlesex University and at the Jackfield Tile Museum at Ironbridge, Shropshire (reserve collection).

Eleanor Greeves 1970-1996

12 Newton Grove, Bedford Park, London W4.

When Eleanor Greeves started making tiles in 1970, few artists were using screen printing as a decorative technique. Over the years, she developed a range of thirty-five designs based on repeating plant motif patterns executed in one or two of ten alternative colors. She also produced nineteen different commemorative tile designs, mainly architectural and based on the buildings surrounding her home in Bedford Park, London. Many of the houses in this area, including Eleanor's own home, were designed by leading Arts & Crafts architects in the late 19th/early 20th century.

Hand screen printed tile with the "Cherry" design, introduced c.1978. 6" square. c.1987. H. & R. Johnson blank. 1,203 examples of this tile were sold. Price group A.

Hand screen printed tile with the "Morning Glory" design, introduced c.1971. 6" square. 1979. H. & R. Johnson blank. 7,326 examples of this tile were sold. Price group A.

Hand screen printed tile with the "Tulip" design. 6" square. c.1980. H. & R. Johnson blank. Price group A.

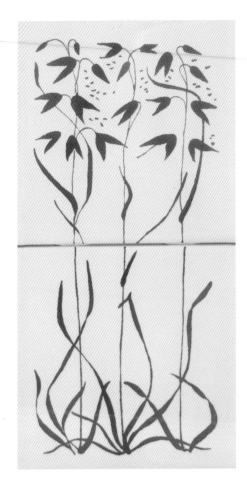

Panel of two hand screen printed tiles with the "Oats" design, introduced 1990. Each tile 4¼" square. c.1990. H. & R. Johnson blanks. 20 sets of this panel were sold. Price group B (panel).

Hand screen printed tile with the "Clematis" design, introduced 1970. 6" square. c.1979. H. & R. Johnson blank. Approximately 1,870 examples of this tile were sold. Price group A.

Hand screen printed tile with the "Columbine" design, introduced 1970. 6" square. c.1982. H. & R. Johnson blank. Approximately 4,310 examples of this tile were sold; it was exhibited at the London Design Centre in April 1971. Price group A.

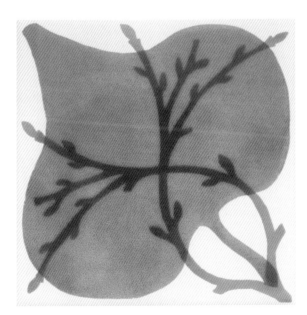

Hand screen printed tile with the "Cornflower" design, introduced 1981. 6" square. c.1982. H. & R. Johnson blank. Approximately 840 examples of this tile were sold. Price group A.

Hand screen printed tile with the "Aspen" design introduced c.1971. 6" square. 1974. H. & R. Johnson blank. Approximately 1,270 examples of this tile were sold; it was exhibited at the London Design Centre May-July 1973. Price group A.

Hand screen printed tile with the "Hawthorn" design, introduced 1971. 6" square. 1973. H. & R. Johnson blank. Approximately 720 examples of this tile were sold. Price group A.

Hand screen printed tile with the "Fuchsia" design, introduced 1986. 6" square. c.1990. H. & R. Johnson blank. Approximately 365 examples of this tile were sold. Price group A.

Hand screen printed tile with the "Daisy" design, introduced 1970. 6" square. 1981. H. & R. Johnson blank. Approximately 1,540 examples of this tile were sold. Price group A.

Hand screen printed tile with the "Marigold" design, introduced c.1971. 6" square. 1988. H. & R. Johnson blank. Approximately 7,080 examples of this tile were sold. Price group A.

Hand screen printed tile with the "Autumn" design. 6" square. c.1990. H. & R. Johnson blank. Approximately 160 examples of this tile were sold. Price group A.

Hand screen printed tile with the "Oak" design, introduced 1970. 6" square. 1970. H. & R. Johnson blank. Price group A.

Hand screen printed tile with the "Bryony" design, introduced 1970. 6" square. 1970. H. & R. Johnson blank. Approximately 105 examples of this tile were sold. Price group A.

Hand screen printed tile with the "Buddleia" design, introduced c.1983. 6" square. c.1990. H. & R. Johnson blank. Approximately 584 examples of this tile were sold. Price group A.

Hand screen printed tile with the "Siciliana" design, introduced c.1975. 6" square. c.1990. H. & R. Johnson blank. Approximately 620 examples of this tile were sold. Price group A.

Hand screen printed tile with the "Traveller's Joy" design, introduced 1979. 6" square. 1979. H. & R. Johnson blank. Approximately 1,865 examples of this tile were sold. Price group A.

Panel of four hand screen printed tiles with the "Summerleas" design, introduced 1981. Each tile 6" square. c.1990. H. & R. Johnson blank. Approximately 545 sets of this panel were sold. Price group B (panel).

Hand screen printed tile with the "Vetch" design, introduced 1972. 6" square. 1972. H. & R. Johnson blank. Approximately 5,760 examples of this tile were sold. Price group A.

Hand screen printed tile with the "Vine" design, introduced 1970. 6" square. 1971. H. & R. Johnson blank. Approximately 1,700 examples of this tile were sold. Price group A.

Hand screen printed tile with the "Turk's Cap Lily" design, introduced 1980. 6" square. 1982. H. & R. Johnson blank. Approximately 650 examples of this tile were sold. Price group A.

Hand screen printed tile with the "Mountain Ash" design, introduced c.1975. 6" square. 1977. H. & R. Johnson blank. Price group A.

Hand screen printed tile with the "Arrow-head" design, introduced 1980. 6" square. 1980. Pilkington's Tiles blank. 2,031 examples of this tile were sold, including a number supplied to the Tate Gallery in London in this special colorway, Khaki on Pilkington's Regency Gold. Price group A.

Panel of two hand screen printed tiles with the "Tudor Rose" design, introduced c.1977. Each tile 6" square. 1977. H. & R. Johnson blanks. 2,177 examples of this panel were sold. Price group B (panel).

Commemorative Tiles

Hand screen printed commemorative tile for the 500th anniversary of William Caxton setting up his press at Westminster in 1476. 6" square. 1975. H. & R. Johnson blank. 630 examples of this tile were sold. Price group B.

Hand screen printed commemorative tile for the 350th anniversary of the death of John Dowland in 1626. 6" square. 1976. H. & R. Johnson blank. 86 examples of this tile were sold. Price group B.

Hand screen printed commemorative tile for the 250th anniversary of the birth of Robert Adam, architect in 1728. 6" square. 1978. H. & R. Johnson blank. 107 examples of this tile were sold. Price group B.

Hand screen printed commemorative tile for the Silver Jubilee of Queen Elizabeth II in 1977. 6" diameter. 1977. H. & R. Johnson blank. 1,233 examples of this tile were sold. Price group B.

Hand screen printed commemorative tile for the 1,000th anniversary of the establishment of the Tynwald, the Isle of Man parliament, in 979A.D. 6" square. 1979. H. & R. Johnson blank. 37 examples of this tile were sold. Price group B.

Hand screen printed commemorative tile for the 100th anniversary of St. Michael and All Angels, Bedford Park, London in 1879. 6" square. 1979. H. & R. Johnson blank. Price group B.

Hand screen printed commemorative tile for the 100th anniversary of the founding of the Old Palace School, Croydon, Surrey in 1889. 6" square. 1989. H. & R. Johnson blank. 665 examples of this tile were sold. Price group B.

Hand screen printed commemorative tile for the wedding of H.R.H. The Price of Wales and Lady Diana Spencer, 29 July 1981. 6" diameter. 1981. H. & R. Johnson blank. 280 examples of this tile were sold. Price group B.

Hand screen printed commemorative tile for the 100th anniversary of St. Peter's Church, Mount Park, Ealing in 1893. 6" square. 1993. H. & R. Johnson blank. 100 examples of this tile were sold. Price group B.

Hand screen printed commemorative tile for the National Trust property, Standen, Sussex. 6" square. 1980. H. & R. Johnson blank. 340 examples of this tile were sold. Price group B.

Bedford Park Tiles

Hand screen printed commemorative tile for the 100th anniversary of the establishment of Bedford Park, London, depicting The Tabard Inn. 6" square. 1975. H. & R. Johnson blank. Price group B.

Hand screen printed commemorative tile from the Bedford Park series "Priory Gardens 1880, Architect E. J. May," design introduced 1985. 6" square. 1983. H. & R. Johnson blank. Price group B.

Hand screen printed commemorative tile from the Bedford Park series "Houses in Queen Anne's Grove by E. J. May," design introduced 1983. 6" square. 1983. H. & R. Johnson blank. Price group B.

Hand screen printed commemorative tile from the Bedford Park series "Houses in Blenheim Road by William Wilson," design introduced 1987. 6" square. c.1987. H. & R. Johnson blank. Price group B.

Hand screen printed commemorative tile from the Bedford Park series "House in Bedford Park designed by E. W. Godwin 1876," design introduced 1987. 6" square. c.1987. H. & R. Johnson blank. Price group B.

Hand screen printed commemorative tile from the Bedford Park series "14 South Parade, Bedford Park, Architect C. F. A. Voysey, built 1891," design introduced 1985. 6" square. 1985. H. & R. Johnson blank. Price group B.

Hand screen printed commemorative tile from the Bedford Park series "Detached house design by R. Norman Shaw R.A.," design introduced 1991. 6" square. 1991. H. & R. Johnson blank. Price group B.

Hand screen printed commemorative tile from the Bedford Park series "The Vicarage, Bedford Park, Architect E. J. May 1881," design introduced 1994. 6" square. 1994. H. & R. Johnson blank. Price group B.

Identification and Marks

Rubber stamp mark on H. & R. Johnson 6" square blank. 1970-1996.

Wendy Guest & Rachel McGurk
Whichford Pottery 1984-2002

Whichford, Shipston on Stour, Warwickshire.

In 1984, Wendy Guest joined the already thriving pottery at Whichford and created the company's first range of decorative tiles. She initially worked at the pottery just two days a week and was joined in 1998 by Rachel McGurk. In January 2003, Wendy and Rachel formed their own company, Delftiles, and are now based at Chipping Norton in Oxfordshire.

Their designs are based on original Dutch and English delftware tiles but these have been developed and changed over the years. Wendy is responsible for the designs, whilst Rachel produces the tiles by hand in a die. The tiles are tin-glazed and hand painted using traditional oxide pigments. The clay body is a red-firing finely grogged clay, which is biscuit fired at approximately 1000°C. Glost firing takes place at a slightly lower temperature in order to achieve a silk finish glaze.

As well as producing a standard range of designs, Wendy and Rachel also work to commission and have undertaken a number of conservation and restoration projects.

Hand painted tin glaze tile depicting a traditional delftware bird design. 5" square. c.2000. *Courtesy of and photograph by Wendy Guest.* Price group A.

Hand painted tin glaze tile depicting a traditional delftware hare design. 5" square. c.2000. *Courtesy of and photograph by Wendy Guest.* Price group A.

Hand painted tin glaze tile depicting a traditional delftware woman with basket design. 5" square. c.2000. *Courtesy of and photograph by Wendy Guest.* Price group A.

Hand painted tin glaze tile depicting a traditional delftware basket of fruit design. 5" square. c.2000. *Courtesy of and photograph by Wendy Guest.* Price group A.

Hand painted tin glaze tile depicting a traditional delftware net loft design. 5" square. c.2000. *Courtesy of and photograph by Wendy Guest.* Price group A.

Identification and Marks
No identifying marks.

Diana Hall
Angus Designs 1979-1993
Diana Hall Ceramics 1993-

1979-1995: Breaky Bottom, Rodmell, Lewes, Sussex
1979-1993: 4 Camden Studios, Camden Street, London N1
1995- : Ann's Cottage, Wimborne St Giles, Dorset

Diana Hall first started working with clay in 1979, learning the fundamentals of pottery from Chris Stevens, a local potter, and Peggy Angus, who had been a major tile designer for *Carter Tiles Ltd.* during the 1960s. Diana and Peggy formed Angus Designs to make tiles decorated by a process that Diana called "Printile Stakfiring." This was essentially a method of printing with oxides onto unglazed commercial floor tiles using polystyrene stamps. The designs were created by Peggy and were based on medieval tapestries.

Another early source of inspiration for Diana was Professor Bobby Baker, one of her tutors at the Royal College of Art, who made replacement medieval inlaid tiles for Winchester Cathedral and Wells Cathedral in the 1970s. Because of her interest in medieval tiles, Diana was approached by Lewes Museum in 1985 to recreate medieval encaustic tiles to be sold through the museum shop. The designs were based on original tiles from nearby Lewes Priory and Diana used local clays from the same sources as the medieval tile makers. The successful development of these handmade tiles has led to her becoming Britain's leading supplier of such tiles for conservation and preservation work.

In 1986, Diana Hall learnt that an original Victorian tile press was to be brought to the Engineerium, an industrial museum situated in nearby Brighton. She was able to persuade the museum to let her have the press on extended loan, enabling her to produce reproductions of Victorian encaustic tiles as well as the medieval replicas.

Illustration from an Angus Designs broadsheet c.1985 showing tiles designed by Peggy Angus and made by Diana Hall utilizing her "Printile Stakfiring" technique. Price group A (each tile).

Angus Designs tea towel illustrating tiles designed by Peggy Angus and made by Diana Hall utilizing her "Printile Stakfiring" technique. Price group A (each tile).

Panel of plastic clay encaustic tiles reproducing medieval designs. Each tile 4" square. c.1985. *Photograph courtesy of Diana Hall.* Price group B (each decorated tile).

Plastic clay encaustic tile reproducing a medieval fleur-de-lis design. 4" square. c.1990. *Courtesy of The British Museum.* Price group B.

"Printile Stakfiring" plastic clay quarry tile depicting a Roman magic word square. 9" square. c.1990. Dennis Ruabon quarry tile blank. *Courtesy of Carolyn Wraight.* Price group B.

Miniature plastic clay encaustic tile reproducing a medieval heraldic lion design from Winchester Cathedral. 2" square. 1998. Price group B.

Frank Hamer
Frank Hamer Ceramics 1982-1995

Llwyn-On, Croes-yn-y-Pant, Mamhilad, via Pontypool, South Wales

From 1982 to about 1995, Frank Hamer produced a number of single, individually painted tiles, making repeats only to order. Many of his tiles were intended for wall hanging and feature an integrated loop in the top of the design or have facilities for a wire frame. He used a blended coarse clay body, biscuit fired at 1000°C and glaze fired at 1280°C. Frank treated the design of these tiles as conventionalized pictures and produced them alongside his other production of decorative functional stonewares.

Frank produced a number of tile murals up to about twenty square feet in size and a number of small pavement designs up to about nine square feet maximum. He also produced some murals for outdoor use; these were painted on commercial, unglazed floor tiles purchased from *George Woolliscroft & Son*. After decoration, these were re-fired to 1100°C.

Frank no longer makes tiles but now concentrates on plates for wall decoration and occasional use. These are almost exclusively decorated with swimming fish.

Set of five hand painted stoneware tiles depicting the "Five Round Houses of Veryan" (Cornwall). Each tile approximately 8" x 6". 1988. *Courtesy of and photograph by Frank Hamer.* Price group C (each).

Two miniature plastic clay encaustic tiles reproducing medieval bird and star designs. Each tile 2" square. 1999. *Courtesy of Maggie Angus Berkowitz.* Price group B.

Hand painted stoneware tile depicting "Chepstow Castle." Approximately 10" x 8". 1988. *Courtesy of and photograph by Frank Hamer.* Price group C.

Identification and Marks
No identifying marks.

Two hand painted stoneware tiles depicting "Grosmont Castle" and "St. Briavels Castle." Each tile approximately 10" x 8". 1988. *Courtesy of and photograph by Frank Hamer.* Price group C (each).

Panel of three hand painted stoneware tiles depicting "Griffithstown, Pontypool." Overall size approximately 18" square. 1988. Made for the Glasgow Garden Festival. *Courtesy of and photograph by Frank Hamer.* Price group E (panel).

Hand painted stoneware tile depicting "Raglan Castle." Approximately 10" x 8". 1988. *Courtesy of and photograph by Frank Hamer.* Price group B.

Set of three hand painted stoneware tiles depicting "Griffithstown, Pontypool." Each tile approximately 8" x 6". 1988. *Courtesy of and photograph by Frank Hamer.* Price Group E (panel)

Panel of forty-five hand painted tiles depicting two trees. Each tile 6" square. 1993. George Woolliscroft & Son blanks. *Courtesy of and photograph by Frank Hamer.* Price group F (panel).

Impressed mark of Frank Hamer's initials. 1982-1995.

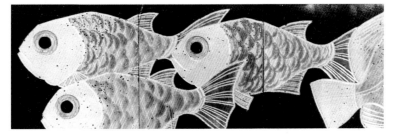

Panel of three hand painted and incised stoneware tiles depicting fish. Each tile 6" square. 1995. *Courtesy of and photograph by Frank Hamer.* Price group D (panel).

Penny Hampson
Penny Hampson Tiles 1985-

1 Unity Street, Hebden Bridge, West Yorkshire

The inspiration for Penny Hampson's handmade tiles comes mainly from the drawings in her sketch book, which she has taken with her on her travels around the world. Although she started making tiles in 1985, it was 1988 before she commenced commercial production and her tile making has been something of an on-and-off occupation over the years. She works in earthenware and stoneware to create press-molded and hand painted tiles, producing a range of standard designs and specials to commission.

The biscuit is fired at temperatures up to 1260°C and Penny uses earthenware glazes fired in a second glost firing. Since 2004, she has been experimenting with carved and decorated brick—a technique that she has successfully employed on a number of major projects.

Press molded plastic clay stoneware tile with a "Persian Fish" design based on a Persian metalwork design from the British Museum. 100mm square. 1988. *Courtesy of and photograph by Penny Hampson.* Price group A.

Two press molded plastic clay stoneware tiles with a design based on a Vermeer painting. Each tile 150mm square. 1988. The right-hand tile has been painted but not glost fired. *Courtesy of and photograph by Penny Hampson.* Price group A (finished tile).

Panel of press molded plastic clay stoneware tiles depicting the Fararfra Oasis. Overall size 450mm square. 1988. *Courtesy of and photograph by Penny Hampson.* Price group C (panel).

A selection of press molded plastic clay stoneware tiles with various designs. Large tiles 150mm square. 1988. *Courtesy of and photograph by Penny Hampson.* Price group A (each tile).

Press molded plastic clay stoneware tile depicting an elephant design influenced by Indian batik on an Oxfam calendar. 150mm square. 1998. *Courtesy of and photograph by Penny Hampson.* Price group B.

Press molded plastic clay stoneware tile depicting sunflowers. 300mm square. 1998. *Courtesy of and photograph by Penny Hampson.* Price group B.

Identification and Marks
  No identifying marks.

References
Finch, Michael. "Traveller's Tiles." *Yorkshire Life Magazine:* 1992

Ernest Heasman (1874-1927)

1918-1927: Harpenden, Hertfordshire

Ernest Heasman was born in Lindfield, Sussex, the fourth and youngest son of a cobbler who died when Ernest was seven. He attended the local village school where the stained glass artist, C. E. Kemp, who also lived in the village, spotted his artistic talent. When Ernest left school, Kemp took him into his studio and taught him the art of painting on glass. The two worked together from 1887 to 1897, during which time Ernest gained a three year scholarship to the Slade School of Art. In 1897, he joined Herbert Bryans' stained glass studio and in 1902 became their chief designer.

After World War I, Ernest established his own studio in Harpenden, Hertfordshire because he felt that stained glass should be a unified art—designed, created, and installed by the artist rather than by a number of different workers. It was during this period that he created most of his decorative tiles, probably using the same pigments as his stained glass work. Some of his tiles appear to be painted on Dutch delftware blanks and he also appears to have used commercial biscuit tile. His tiles were produced for domestic and church settings and to commemorate personal occasions.

Hand painted over-glaze tile depicting "Cancer," from a series of zodiac designs. 5" square. 1920s. Dutch delftware blank. *Private collection.* Price group B.

Hand painted over-glaze tile depicting "Virgo," from a series of zodiac designs. 5" square. 1920s. Dutch delftware blank. *Private collection.* Price group B.

Hand painted over-glaze tile with the motto "All seasons and their change all please alike." 5" square. 1920s. Dutch delftware blank. *Private collection.* Price group B.

Hand painted over-glaze tile depicting "Libra," from a series of zodiac designs. 5" square. 1920s. Dutch delftware blank. *Private collection.* Price group B.

Hand painted over-glaze tile depicting "The Clock House." 5" square. 1920s. Dutch delftware blank. *Private collection.* Price group C.

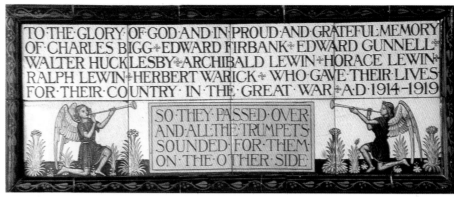

Panel of eight hand painted over-glaze tiles commemorating servicemen who died in the Great War 1914-1919, from the Methodist Church, Batford, Hertfordshire. Each tile 4" x 6". c.1920. Unknown commercial blanks. *Photograph courtesy of Linette O'Sullivan.*

Hand painted over-glaze tile depicting "Spring." 5" square. 1920s. Dutch delftware blank. *Private collection.* Price group C.

Detail of Batford War Memorial panel. *Photograph courtesy of Linette O'Sullivan.*

Hand painted over-glaze tile depicting King David from St. John's Church, Harpenden, Hertfordshire. 8" square. 1920s. Unknown commercial blank. *Photograph courtesy of Linette O'Sullivan.* Price group D.

Identification and Marks

Some of the tiles are signed "EH" or "AEH" for Alfred Ernest Heasman.

Eileen Hemsoll 1968-2001

18 Mead Rise, Edgbaston, Birmingham

Eileen Hemsoll is an artist who produced a number of tile pictures but more recently has returned to her main interest of painting. She used an unusual technique, employing enamels ground-laid onto pre-glazed commercial white tiles. Outlines and details were then scratched back through to the white glaze in a technique akin to sgraffito. The tiles were fired to 780°C.

Panel of eight hand painted over-glaze tiles depicting fish and a mermaid. Each tile 6" square in original frame. 1990s. Unknown commercial blanks. *Courtesy of and photograph by Eileen Hemsoll*. Price group C (panel).

Identification and Marks

Eileen M. Hemsoll

Painted signature used on the front of tiles. 1968-2001.

Douglas Hunter
Hunter Art & Tile Studio 1982-

1982-1985: Paisley, Scotland
1985- : Harestanes, Ancrum, Roxburghshire, Scotland

Douglas Hunter started his ceramic tile business in 1982, when he took over the back-court wash-house behind his Paisley flat as a studio-cum-workshop. As a child growing up in and around his native Glasgow, he was always fascinated by the richly tiled "walley closes" (hallways) and stairwells in many of the old tenement buildings. He also discovered the many dairy and butcher shop interiors decorated with tiles made by the local firm of J. Duncan & Co. The rich glazes and tube-lined designs of their tiles have always been an inspiration to him.

Three tube-lined tiles depicting flowers, designed and made by Douglas Hunter. Center tile 8" x 4", others 6" x 3". 1980s/90s. H. & R. Johnson blanks. *Courtesy of Douglas Hunter. Photograph by JLP Systems*. Price group A (each).

Panel of nine hand painted over-glaze tiles depicting "Europa and the Bull." Each tile 6" square in original frame. 1990s. Unknown commercial blanks. *Courtesy of and photograph by Eileen Hemsoll*. Price group C (panel).

Panel of four hand painted over-glaze tiles depicting rugby players. Each tile 6" square in original frame. 1990s. Unknown commercial blanks. *Courtesy of and photograph by Eileen Hemsoll*. Price group B (panel).

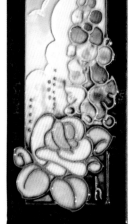

The Hunter Art & Tile Studio is very much a family workshop, with Douglas's wife Charlotte, sister Karen, and son Richard all contributing at various times. Many of Douglas's designs are based on tiles from the Art Nouveau period and he has also adapted designs by Charles Rennie Macintosh, the renowned Glasgow architect.

The workshop uses biscuit tile bought in from *H. & R. Johnson Ltd.* and *H. & E. Smith Ltd.* and occasionally produces its own biscuit tiles. Many of the tube-lined designs are embellished with under-glaze brushwork, much in the style of J. Duncan & Co. A large proportion of their output is sold through a number of top retail galleries and the studio also undertakes commissions for tile panels and specials to order.

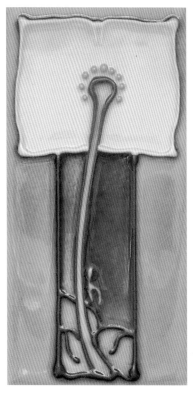

Tube-lined tile with an Art Nouveau inspired floral design, made by Douglas Hunter. 6" x 3". c.1985. H. & R. Johnson blank. Price group A.

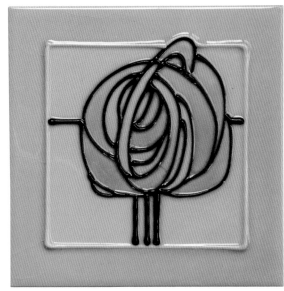

Tube-lined tile with a Charles Rennie Mackintosh inspired design. 6" square. c.1990. H. & R. Johnson blank. *Courtesy of Mary Bentley.* Price group A.

Three tube-lined tiles with Charles Rennie Mackintosh inspired designs. Center tile 8" x 4", others 6" x 3". 1990s. H. & R. Johnson blanks. *Courtesy of Douglas Hunter. Photograph by JLP Systems.* Price group A (each).

Panel of two tube-lined tiles with "Still Life" design by Douglas Hunter. Each tile 8" x 6". 1980s. H. & R. Johnson blanks. *Courtesy of Douglas Hunter. Photograph by JLP Systems.* Price group B (panel).

Panel of four tube-lined tiles depicting "Capricorn," from a series of zodiac designs by Richard Hunter. Each tile 4" square. 1990s. H. & R. Johnson blanks. *Courtesy of Douglas Hunter. Photograph by JLP Systems.* Price group C (panel).

Panel of eleven tube-lined tiles depicting a "Medieval Ship," designed by Douglas Hunter. Center tile 6" square. 1990s. H. & R. Johnson blanks. *Courtesy of Douglas Hunter. Photograph by JLP Systems.* Price group D (panel).

Panel of eleven tube-lined tiles depicting a "Thames Sailing Barge," designed by Douglas Hunter. Center tile 6" square. 1990s. H. & R. Johnson blanks. *Courtesy of Douglas Hunter. Photograph by JLP Systems.* Price group D (panel).

Two tube-lined tiles depicting a green woman and a green man, designed by Douglas Hunter. Each tile 6" square. 1990s. H. & R. Johnson blanks. *Courtesy of Douglas Hunter. Photograph by JLP Systems.* Price group B (each).

Panel of eight tube-lined tiles depicting a "Roman Lady," designed by Richard Hunter. Large tiles 6" square. 1990s. H. & R. Johnson blanks. *Courtesy of Douglas Hunter. Photograph by JLP Systems.* Price group C (panel).

Panel of four tube-lined tiles depicting an "English Longhorn Cow," designed by Charlotte Hunter. Each tile 6" square. 1990s. H. & R. Johnson blanks. *Courtesy of Douglas Hunter. Photograph by JLP Systems.* Price group C (panel).

Panel of nine tube-lined tiles depicting a "Pig," designed by Richard and Charlotte Hunter. Each tile 4" square. 1990s. H. & R. Johnson blanks. *Courtesy of Douglas Hunter. Photograph by JLP Systems.* Price group C (panel).

Panel of nine tube-lined tiles depicting an "Ice Cream Cone," designed by Charlotte Hunter. Each tile 3" square. 1990s. H. & R. Johnson blanks. *Courtesy of Douglas Hunter. Photograph by JLP Systems.* Price group C (panel).

Identification and Marks

Tube-lined tile depicting a "Dairy Cow" in the style of J. Duncan & Co., designed by Karen Hunter. 8" square. 1988. H. & R. Johnson blank. *Courtesy of Douglas Hunter. Photograph by JLP Systems.* Price group B.

Hunter Art & Tile Studio

Harestanes, Ancrum, Jedburgh, Roxburghshire

Tel. Ancrum (08353) 328

Self-adhesive label used since 1985. In addition, most of Douglas Hunter's tiles are signed with an "h" on the front.

Pat Hyatt
Gus & Pat Hyatt Ceramics 1992-

82 Richmond Park Road, Kingston-upon-Thames, Surrey

Pat Hyatt has been decorating tiles since 1992 and designed a series of ranges for bathroom use for Color 1 Ceramics in Richmond Road, East Twickenham, Middlesex. These were produced in quite large numbers up until about 2000, but in lesser numbers since then. Pat decorates on white gloss tiles, repainting them with brush-on glaze. The tiles are then re-fired to 990°C for approximately ten hours using an electric kiln. Repeat designs are produced by using tracings.

Pat also exhibited a number of one-off designs at various art and craft shows. She has used a range of different British commercial blanks over the years but more recently has been using tiles from Ceres Ceramics in Italy.

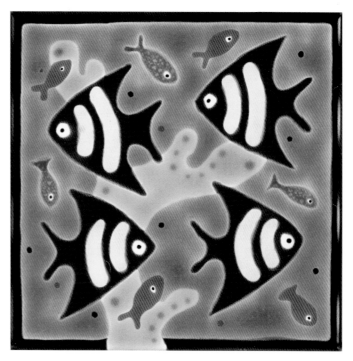

Hand painted over-glaze tile with a fish design. 6" square. 1990s. Unknown commercial blank. *Courtesy of and photograph by Pat Hyatt.* Price group A.

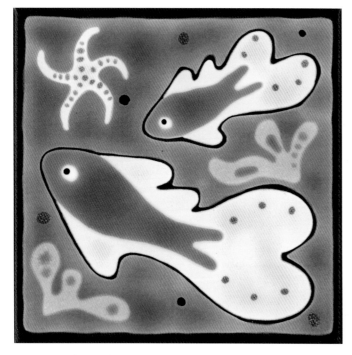

Hand painted over-glaze tile with a fish design. 6" square. 1990s. Unknown commercial blank. *Courtesy of and photograph by Pat Hyatt.* Price group A.

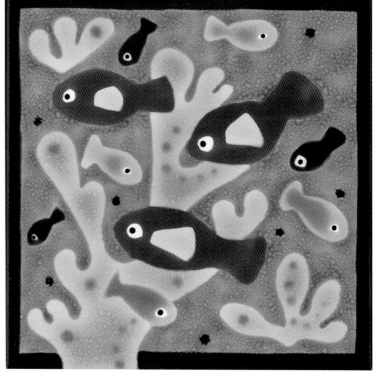

Hand painted over-glaze tile with a fish design. 6" square. 1990s. Unknown commercial blank. *Courtesy of and photograph by Pat Hyatt.* Price group A.

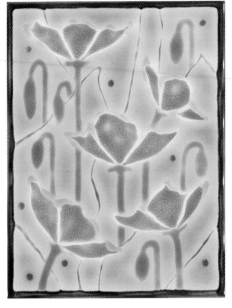

Hand painted over-glaze tile with a floral design. 8" x 6". 1990s. Unknown commercial blank. *Courtesy of and photograph by Pat Hyatt.* Price group A.

Hand painted over-glaze tile with a floral design. 6" square. 1990s. Unknown commercial blank. *Courtesy of and photograph by Pat Hyatt.* Price group A.

Identification and Marks
No identifying marks.

Noreen Jaafar & Jonathan Martin
Jaafar Designs 1994-

The Old Rectory, 68 Kingshill Road, Dursley, Gloucestershire

Noreen Jaafar and her husband Jonathan Martin have been making tiles since 1994 and have developed their own "Persian" alkaline glaze that enables them to produce tiles with vibrant deep glossy colors and designs. The rich blue, green, and turquoise colors were initially painted onto *H. & R. Johnson Ltd.* biscuit tiles, but since 2000 Noreen and Jonathan have used B.C.T.'s *Candy* biscuit. Designs include a sea life series with fish, sea horses, and dolphins and a range of geometric designs. They also undertake commissions.

Hand glaze painted tile depicting two tropical fish. 3" x 6". c.2000. H. & R. Johnson blank. Price group A.

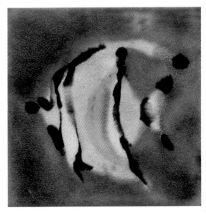

Hand glaze painted tile depicting an angelfish. 150mm square. c.2000. B.C.T. Candy Cornite blank. Price group A.

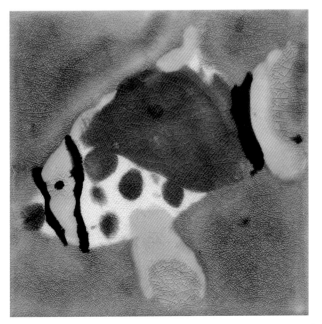

Hand glaze painted tile depicting a tropical fish. 150mm square. c.2000. B.C.T. Candy Cornite blank. Price group A.

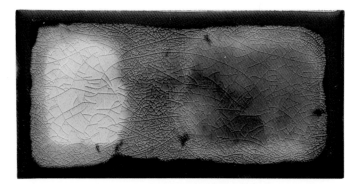

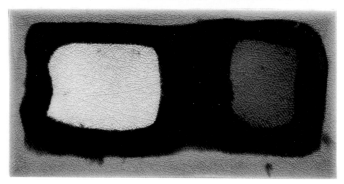

Two hand glaze painted tiles from the "Florida Square" range. Each tile 75mm x 150mm. 1999. B.C.T. Candy Cornite blanks. The Florida Square range won first prize for Best British Wall Tile, at Expotile 1999. Price group A (each).

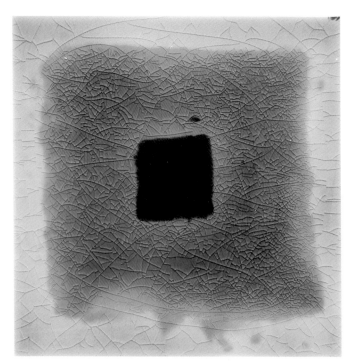

Hand glaze painted tile from the "Florida Square" range. 150mm square. 1999. Mosa (The Netherlands) blank. Price group A.

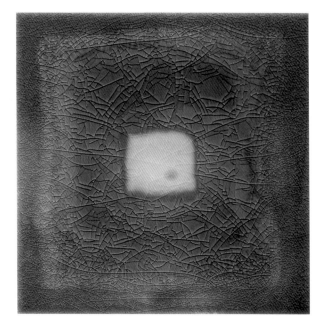

Hand glaze painted tile from the "Florida Square" range. 150mm square. 1999. Mosa (The Netherlands) blank. Price group A.

Identification and Marks
No identifying marks.

Ceri Elisabeth Jones
Cat on a Hot Tile Roof 1993-1998

6 Walston Road, Wenvoe, Cardiff, Wales

Ceri Elisabeth Jones graduated in English but later attended Carmarthen College of Technology & Art, where she took an Arts Foundation course. She became interested in ceramics when she joined Gwili Pottery, Pontarsais, near Carmarthen, where she was taught by Pru Green. She left in 1993 to establish her own business, Cat on a Hot Tile Roof, where she specialized in decorating tiles and tile panels.

Hand painted cuerda seca tile with a seascape design. 6" square. c.1995. H. & R. Johnson blank. *Courtesy of Roger Hensman.* Price group A.

Initially, Ceri made her own blanks but found this very time consuming and soon started to purchase blanks from *H. & R. Johnson Ltd.*, which she hand painted, occasionally using wax-resist outlines. Most of her work was originally commissioned but some of these she was asked to repeat a number of times. Her tiles were fired in her own electric kiln at 1220°C.

In 1998, Ceri went to work for a pottery in New Zealand where she now specializes in design.

Identification and Marks

Sometimes marked with her initials "CEJ" or a monogram of "C" and "J".

David Lloyd Jones (b.1928-d.1994) 1962-1994

Fulford House, 45 Fulford, York, Yorkshire

David Lloyd Jones was best known as a studio potter working with reduced stonewares fired at high temperatures. His work is distinctively dark and abstract, with the design being painted in oxides and glazes against an unglazed stoneware background. During the 1970s, he produced a small number of stoneware tiles and tile murals, all of which were created on his own stoneware biscuit.

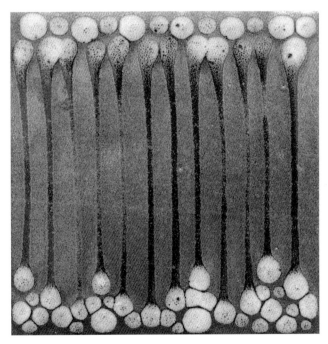

Hand painted stoneware tile with an abstract design. 6" square. 1975. Price group C.

Identification and Marks

David Lloyd Jones used a small, square, impressed mark of his full name in three lines: "DAVID/LLOYD/JONES."

Robert Jones
Jones's Tiles 1979-

Manor Barn, Orleton, Ludlow, Shropshire

Working in the traditional tin-glaze technique, Robert Jones has taken his inspiration from traditional Dutch and English delftware tiles. In addition to creating faithful reproductions of the original tiles, Robert has sought to introduce more contemporary motifs into his work. He has produced blue and manganese monochrome tiles as well as polychrome bird tiles based on those made at Liverpool in the 1750s and at Lambeth in the 1730s. Unique to Robert's range are re-creations of some of the printed tiles produced at Liverpool from 1756 onwards. These include single color designs based on the earlier Aesop's Fables tiles as well as the neo-classical vase designs done by Guy Green in the 1780s. Recent developments include a series of gothic animals in rich browns and reds, a French rose trellis repeating design, and a more contemporary series of farm animals. He produces a standard range of designs for sale in the U.S.A., where they are marketed as the "Elon Palace Collection."

Robert uses biscuit tile made especially for him by *H. & E. Smith Ltd.* and fires the tin-glazed tiles to 1040°C.

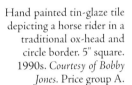

Hand painted tin-glaze tile depicting a horse rider in a traditional ox-head and circle border. 5" square. 1990s. *Courtesy of Bobby Jones.* Price group A.

Hand painted tin-glaze tile depicting a rabbit, with traditional ox-head corners. 5" square. 1990s. *Courtesy of Bobby Jones.* Price group A.

Hand painted tin-glaze tile depicting a flower vase in a traditional London carnation and powdered manganese octagon border. 5″ square. 1990s. *Courtesy of Bobby Jones.* Price group A.

Hand painted tin-glaze tile depicting a polychrome flower vase with traditional London spider-head corners. 5″ square. 1990s. *Courtesy of Bobby Jones.* Price group A.

Hand painted tin-glaze tile depicting a polychrome bird with traditional fleur-de-lys corners. 5″ square. 1990s. *Courtesy of Bobby Jones.* Price group A.

Hand painted tin-glaze tile depicting a polychrome bird in a traditional Liverpool barbed accolade border. 5" square. 1990s. *Courtesy of Bobby Jones.* Price group A.

Hand painted tin-glaze tile depicting a polychrome flower basket with modern corner ornaments. 5" square. 1990s. *Courtesy of Bobby Jones.* Price group A.

Printed tin-glaze tile with an all-over daisy pattern, a re-creation of a Guy Green design from the 1780s. 5" square. 1990s. *Courtesy of Bobby Jones.* Price group A.

Hand painted tin-glaze tile depicting a pig, with traditional ox-head corners. 5" square. 1990s. *Courtesy of Bobby Jones.* Price group A.

Printed tin-glaze tile depicting a rural scene in a rococo border. 5" square. 1990s. *Courtesy of Bobby Jones.* Price group A.

Hand painted tin-glaze tile depicting pigs. 5" square. 1990s. *Courtesy of Bobby Jones.* Price group A.

Printed tin-glaze tile depicting a rural scene in a rococo border. 5" square. 1990s. *Courtesy of Bobby Jones.* Price group A.

Hand painted gold luster tin-glaze tile with a foliate design in a quadrate with checkered corners. 5" square. 1990s. *Courtesy of Bobby Jones.* Price group B.

Hand painted tin-glaze tile depicting gooseberries, with modern corner ornaments. 5" square. 1990s. *Courtesy of Bobby Jones.* Price group A.

Panel of four printed tin-glaze tiles with a design based on a Malvern medieval tile. Each tile 3" square. 1990s. *Courtesy of Bobby Jones.* Price group B (panel).

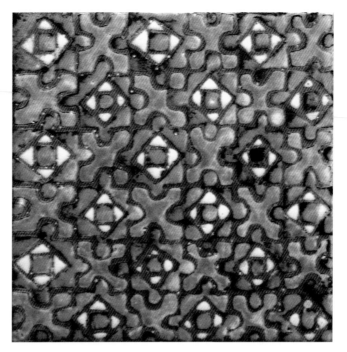

Hand painted wax resist stoneware tile with a geometric design. 6" square. 1990s. *Courtesy of and photograph by Colin Kellam.* Price group A.

Identification and Marks

No identifying marks on tiles for the U.K. market, but a rubber stamp incorporating the words "Elon Palace Collection" is used on tiles exported to the U.S.A.

Colin Kellam 1969-

South Street, Totnes, Devon

Colin Kellam's introduction to pottery came while he was working as an apprentice with Marianne de Trey at Shinner's Bridge Pottery, Dartington, Devon, from 1961-1969. He then went on to establish his own pottery in Totnes, where he works with a skilled team of throwers and decorators producing a large range of domestic ware together with imposing animal sculptures.

Colin's first tiles were based on traditional Islamic zillij cut tile work and were decorated in bold colors. The individual shapes were fitted together to create large-scale mosaic panels. These early tiles were made from plastic clay, hand rolled and cut to shape, but in the early 1990s he constructed his own ram press for tile making, which ensured a flatter and more even product. Colin works in stoneware and decorates his tiles and pottery with cobalt, chrome, vanadium, and manganese oxides, fired in his own home-built oil-burning kiln at temperatures in excess of 1300°C. He specializes in single tiles but occasionally undertakes commissions for larger panels. His design motifs are chiefly fish, plants, cockerels, hares, and ducks, plus occasional geometric designs. Most of his decorative output has been made since 1995.

Hand painted wax resist stoneware tile depicting an elephant. 6" square. 1990s. *Courtesy of Freddie & Annie Taggart.* Price group A.

Hand painted wax resist stoneware tile depicting a rabbit. 6" square. 1990s. *Courtesy of Freddie & Annie Taggart.* Price group A.

Hand painted wax resist stoneware tile depicting fish. 6" square. 1990s. *Courtesy of and photograph by Colin Kellam.* Price group A.

Hand painted wax resist stoneware tile depicting a circle of fish. 6" square. 1990s. *Courtesy of Roger Hensman.* Price group A.

Hand painted wax resist stoneware tile depicting a cockerel. 6" square. 1990s. *Courtesy of Freddie & Annie Taggart.* Price group A.

Hand painted stoneware tile depicting fish. 6" square. 1990s. *Courtesy of and photograph by Colin Kellam.* Price group A.

Hand painted wax resist stoneware tile depicting a hen. 6" square. 1990s. *Courtesy of and photograph by Colin Kellam.* Price group A.

Hand painted wax resist stoneware tile depicting fish. 6" square. 1990s. *Courtesy of and photograph by Colin Kellam.* Price group A.

Hand painted wax resist stoneware tile depicting a duck. 6" square. 1990s. *Courtesy of and photograph by Colin Kellam.* Price group A.

Hand painted stoneware tile depicting snowdrops. 6" square. 1990s. *Courtesy of and photograph by Colin Kellam.* Price group A.

Hand painted wax resist stoneware tile depicting a duck. 6" square. 1990s. *Courtesy of and photograph by Colin Kellam.* Price group A.

Hand painted stoneware tile depicting cherries. 6" square. 1990s. *Courtesy of and photograph by Colin Kellam.* Price group A.

Hand painted stoneware tile depicting a fuchsia. 6" square. 1990s. *Courtesy of and photograph by Colin Kellam.* Price group A.

Hand painted wax resist stoneware tile depicting a duck. 6" square. 1990s. Price group A.

Hand painted wax resist stoneware tile depicting honeysuckle. 6" square. 1990s. Price group A.

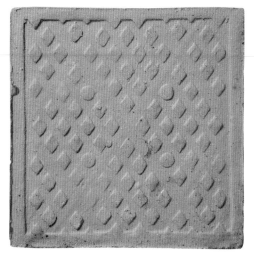

Plastic clay stoneware wall tile. 6" square. The distinctive back of this tile was produced by the ram press that Colin built in the early 1990s. *Courtesy of Roger Hensman.*

Plastic clay stoneware wall tile. 6" square. This is a later pattern of back used by Colin Kellam from c. 2000.

Rebecca Landrock & Patrice Hamilton
The Village Pottery Ltd. 1984-

Clark's Village, Street, Somerset.

Rebecca Landrock started making tiles in 1984 while she was a student at Camberwell College of Art. She is now working in partnership with Patrice Hamilton producing hand painted tiles. Early products were produced on Rebecca's own handmade blanks marked "Rebecca Ball" (her maiden name) but current production is on pre-glazed *Pilkington's Tiles Ltd.* blanks. Rebecca and Patrice use brush-on glazes applied to the pre-glazed tile and re-fired to 1040°C. They produce a standard range of designs and will also undertake small-scale hand painted tile murals. Most of their tiles are made up into pot stands using a cork backing and they also have a series of framed tiles and hob covers (nine tiles set on a solid base with a natural pine edge).

Hand painted tile depicting bath time, pattern no. SPT6. 6" square. c.1999. Pilkington's Tiles blank. *Courtesy of Rebecca Landrock.* Price group A.

Hand painted tile depicting a rabbit, pattern no. TS106. 6" square in original cork trivet. 1994. Pilkington's Tiles blank. Price group A.

Hand painted tile depicting a man and a woman. 6" square. c.1999. Pilkington's Tiles blank. *Courtesy of Rebecca Landrock.* Price group A.

Hand painted tile depicting fish. 6" square. c.1999. Pilkington's Tiles blank. *Courtesy of Rebecca Landrock.* Price group A.

Hand painted tile depicting a hen. 6" square. c.1999. Pilkington's Tiles blank. *Courtesy of Rebecca Landrock.* Price group A.

Hand painted tile depicting a dog, pattern no. TS102. 6" square. c.1999. Pilkington's Tiles blank. *Courtesy of Rebecca Landrock.* Price group A.

Identification and Marks

HAND-PAINTED CERAMIC TILES
For people who appreciate quality and individuality. Decorative and fun, heat-resistant and durable – to clean simply wipe over with a damp cloth.

The Village Pottery
Clarks Village STREET Somerset BA16 0BB
Telephone 01458 443889

Made in England

Self-adhesive label. 1984-

Painted mark used on tiles decorated by Patrice Hamilton.

Bernard Leach (b.1887-d.1979)
The Leach Pottery 1920-1972

St Ives, Cornwall

Bernard Leach was born in Hong Kong and raised in Japan by his grandparents. He came to England to attend school at the age of ten, and after a brief spell working as a clerk for the Hong Kong and Shanghai Bank, he studied art at the London School of Art. In 1909, he returned to Japan to teach etching, a technique that he had learnt from Frank Brangwyn, and eventually met up with the talented Japanese potter, Shoji Hamada in 1919. In 1920, the two of them came to England and established The Leach Pottery at St Ives. Hamada stayed with Leach for three years before returning to Japan.

Leach was strongly influenced by oriental pottery and this is reflected in much of his work. He was always experimenting, particularly with kilns, and eventually constructed his famous "Climbing Kiln" in which he was able to reach stoneware temperatures using wood as a fuel. Leach is best known for his pots decorated with dark oxide colors, chiefly iron and cobalt, with landscapes in Korean and Japanese style. The Pottery also produced quite large numbers of simply decorated 4" and 6" tiles for fireplaces using similar techniques and designs to his pots. Many of these tiles are signed with his stylized monogram on the front and are often impressed in the coarse stoneware back of the tile with "The St Ives Seal."

During the 1960s and 1970s, Leach decorated some commercial blanks sourced from *Candy Tiles Ltd.*, which he refired at stoneware temperatures. He also produced a number of tile panels, usually consisting of four 9" tiles depicting tigers and other oriental creatures; these were often mounted in wrought iron frames.

Hand painted stoneware tile depicting a Korean landscape. 4" square. c.1950. Price group D.

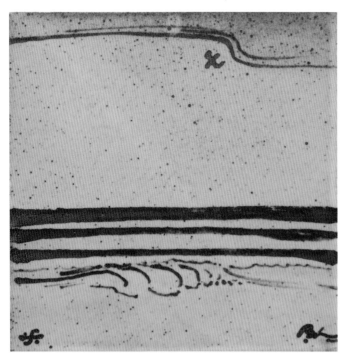

Hand painted tile depicting a seascape. 6" square. 1957. Candy & Co. floor tile blank. *Courtesy of Eric Mellon.* Price group D.

Impressed "St. Ives" mark on 4" stoneware blank.

Painted "St. Ives" mark sometimes found on the front of tiles.

Hand painted stoneware tile depicting a deer. 4" square. c.1950. *Courtesy of Carolyn Wraight.* Price group D.

Painted initials "BL" for Bernard Leach.

Philip & Frannie Leach
Springfield Pottery 1979-

88 Springfield, Hartland, North Devon

Philip Leach was born in 1947 at Alton in Hampshire, and from 1949 to 1956 lived with his father, Michael Leach, next door to his grandfather, Bernard Leach's Pottery at St Ives in Cornwall. He attended Barnstaple Grammar School from 1958-1966 and then attended Newton Park Teacher Training College, taking art and design as his main subjects. After working for a year in Paddington, London, as a teacher, he traveled to Iran and taught at the American Community School. In 1976, he returned to England and worked with his father for three months before joining his brother-in-law, Clive Bowen, in his pottery.

In March 1977, Philip married Frannie, who was working for his father, and in 1979 they established the Springfield Pottery. They built their own kiln from instructions in one of Daniel Rhodes' books and decided to make earthenwares. The early days were difficult, and to supplement their income Philip taught pottery for eight years at The Small School in Hartland. In 1996, Philip undertook a short lecture tour to Japan and in 1998 held a major exhibition there.

Philip and Frannie have a Victorian fly press with which they produce hand-pressed tiles, some featuring impressed designs. They have a small standard range and also produce a number of specials to commission. They also work with brushed, slip-trailed, feathered, and sgraffito techniques and in the past have experimented with silk-screening and encaustic tiles. Because they work in plastic clay, all the tiles are pressed twice and turned in the drying process to avoid warping.

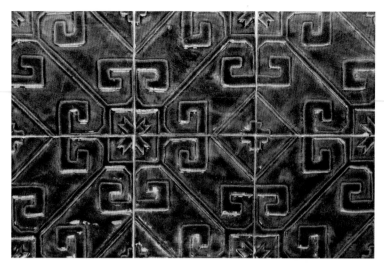

Panel of six relief molded tiles, "Persian." Each tile 4" square. 1990s. The design was impressed from a wood block and glazed with a copper blue glaze. *Courtesy of and photograph by Philip & Frannie Leach.* Price group A (each tile).

Relief molded tile, "Birds." 6" square. 1990s. The design was impressed from a lino cut and glazed with a copper glaze. *Courtesy of and photograph by Philip & Frannie Leach.* Price group A.

Panel of six relief molded tiles, "Japanese Signature." Each tile 4" square. 1990s. The design was impressed from a wood block and glazed with a copper glaze. *Courtesy of and photograph by Philip & Frannie Leach.* Price group A (each tile).

Relief molded and hand painted tile, "Flamingo." 6" square. 1990s. The design was impressed from a wood block and glazed with a lead bisulphide glaze. *Courtesy of and photograph by Philip & Frannie Leach.* Price group A.

Relief molded tile, "Bear Rock, Hartland." 6" square. 1990s. The design was impressed from a wood block and glazed with a copper glaze. *Courtesy of and photograph by Philip & Frannie Leach.* Price group A.

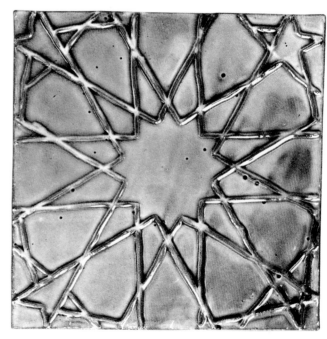

Relief molded tile, "Islamic Star." 6" square. 1990s. The design was impressed from a wood block and glazed with a copper glaze. *Courtesy of and photograph by Philip & Frannie Leach.* Price group A.

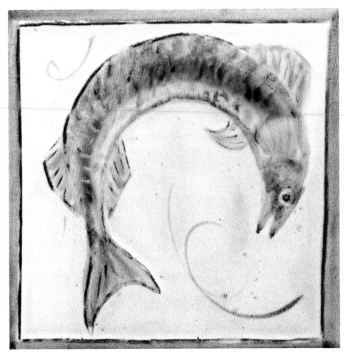

Relief molded tile, "Mackerel." 6" square. 1990s. The design was impressed from a wood block and glazed with a borax glaze. *Courtesy of and photograph by Philip & Frannie Leach.* Price group A.

Combed slip tile with an abstract design. 6" square. 1990s. *Courtesy of and photograph by Philip & Frannie Leach.* Price group A.

Panel of two glazed encaustic and two plain tiles with a heraldic griffin design. Each tile 4" square. 1990s. *Courtesy of and photograph by Philip & Frannie Leach.* Price group A (each decorated tile).

Relief molded and hand painted tile, "Toe-Picking Bird." 6" square. 1990s. The design was impressed from a wood block and glazed with a borax glaze. *Courtesy of and photograph by Philip & Frannie Leach.* Price group A.

Slip trailed tile with an abstract design. 6" square. 1990s. *Courtesy of and photograph by Philip & Frannie Leach.* Price group A.

Identification and Marks

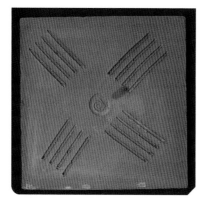

Impressed mark and incised lines used on plastic clay wall tiles.

Jo Lester
Isle of Wight Pottery 1953-c.1985

Freshwater, Isle of Wight

Born in April 1912, Jo Lester was injured during World War II, leaving him unable to pursue his career. In 1951, he therefore decided to turn his hobby of making pottery into a business. Two years later, he moved to the Isle of Wight and established the Isle of Wight Pottery at Freshwater, producing a wide range of pottery decorated with banding and sgraffito designs, mainly featuring animals, birds, and flowers.

During the early 1970s, Jo produced a small range of decorated tiles, using the same sgraffito technique applied to *H. & R. Johnson Ltd.* blanks. These are usually unmarked, although Jo's hand-thrown pottery is stamped with a mark consisting of his Christian name "Jo" over "I.O.W." within an outline map of the island. This mark may also have been used on tiles. Jo stopped potting in the mid-1980s.

Hand painted and sgraffito tile depicting a cockerel. 6" square. 1967. Richards Tiles blank. Price group A.

Hand painted and sgraffito tile with a floral design. 6" square. 1960. Richards Tiles blank. Price group A.

Identification and Marks

Printed mark used on pots. It is possible that this mark was also used on tiles.

Kay Lockie
Palm Pottery 1989-

Bois Avenue, Chesham Bois, Amersham, Buckinghamshire

Kay Lockie first became interested in pottery whilst living in Dubai, where she attended classes and learnt how to make and decorate pots. On her return to England in 1989, she and her husband bought a house in Buckinghamshire and her husband suggested that she make tiles for a new kitchen they were having installed. A number of friends saw the tiles she had made and asked her to make some for them, so Palm Pottery was born.

Kay has made a wide variety of different tiles over the years, specializing mainly in on-glaze decoration of commercial tiles. This enables her to supply clients with hand painted decorative tiles and panels to match commercial field tiles. She has also produced a variety of different shaped tiles, including some rather unusual designs for the reception area of the Coca-Cola Co. headquarters in Slough, Berkshire. These were produced in the company colors of red, gold, and yellow. Other techniques have included molded raised-line tiles in imitation of tube-lining, and sgraffito.

Panel of sixteen hand stenciled tiles depicting fruits. Each tile 4" square. 1990s. *Courtesy of and photograph by Kay Lockie.* Price group A (each decorated tile).

Panel of relief molded and hand painted tiles depicting fruits with a floral border. Each fruit tile 4" square. 1990s. *Courtesy of and photograph by Kay Lockie.* Price group A (each decorated tile).

Detail of panel of hand painted tiles depicting penguins. Each tile 6" square. 1990s. *Courtesy of and photograph by Kay Lockie.* Price group C (panel).

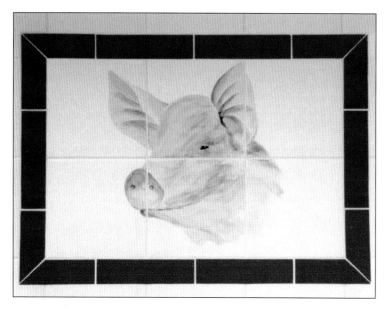

Panel of six hand painted tiles depicting a pig. Each tile 6" square. 1990s. *Courtesy of and photograph by Kay Lockie.* Price group C (panel).

Panel of six hand painted tiles depicting a sheep. Each tile 6" square. 1990s. *Courtesy of and photograph by Kay Lockie.* Price group C (panel).

Panel of thirty-six hand painted tiles depicting the logo of Chartridge Golf Club. Each tile 6" square. 1990s. *Courtesy of and photograph by Kay Lockie.* Price group D (panel).

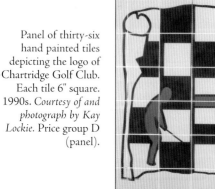

Sgraffito tile with a fourfold fleur-de-lis design. 4" square. 1990s. Price group A.

Press molded plastic clay border tile with a geometric design. 3" x 6". 1990s. Price group A.

Set of three press molded plastic clay border tiles with a fish design. Each tile 3" x 6". 1990s. Price group A (each).

Identification and Marks

Individual tiles are not normally marked, but some commissioned panels have been signed at the request of the client.

Andrew McGarva & Clare Casson 1982-1989

Wobage Farm, Upton Bishop, Ross on Wye, Herefordshire

Andrew McGarva began making tiles in 1982, utilizing *Hereford Tiles Ltd.* blanks that he decorated and re-fired to stoneware temperature. His wife, Clare Casson, joined him in 1986 and, using Andrew's motifs, changed the production over to tin-glaze, painted onto *H. & R. Johnson Ltd.* blanks. This was necessitated by the closure of Hereford Tiles' own tile production facilities. Andrew and Clare stopped making tiles in 1989, but their designs were adapted to screen printing and hand coloring and continued to be produced by *Fired Earth*, who had marketed their tiles. Andrew and Clare continue to make pots and are now based at La Tuilerie, Aunay-en-Bazois, in France.

Andrew was responsible for the original stoneware designs featuring animals, while Clare designed the flowers and birds series that were only produced in tin-glaze. At the height of their business, they employed three part-time painters. They also produced a number of site-specific commissions.

Hand painted tile depicting a cat. 6" square. 1980s. Unknown commercial blank. *Courtesy of and photograph by Andrew McGarva & Clare Casson.* Price group A.

Hand painted tile depicting a peacock. 6" square. 1980s. Unknown commercial blank. *Courtesy of and photograph by Andrew McGarva & Clare Casson.* Price group A.

Hand painted tile depicting a cow. 6" square. 1980s. Unknown commercial blank. *Courtesy of and photograph by Andrew McGarva & Clare Casson.* Price group A.

Hand painted tile depicting a hen. 6" square. 1980s. Shaw Hereford blank. *Private collection.* Price group A.

Hand painted tile depicting a ram. 6" square. 1980s. Shaw Hereford blank. *Private collection.* Price group A.

Hand painted tile depicting a carnation. 6" square. 1980s. Unknown commercial blank. *Courtesy of and photograph by Andrew McGarva & Clare Casson.* Price group A.

Identification and Marks

Although their standard designs were not signed, site specific commissions were usually signed "C Casson" or "AM."

Panel of sixteen hand painted tiles depicting a vase of flowers. Each tile 6" square. 1980s. Unknown commercial blanks. *Courtesy of and photograph by Andrew McGarva & Clare Casson.* Price group D (panel).

Gesine Mahoney 1987-2005

Unit 2, School Close, St Columb Minor, Newquay, Cornwall

Gesine Mahoney studied art in Bremen, Germany, where she achieved a number of awards for her graphic designs. Her artistic works range from graphic art illustration to painting and sculpture and, since 1987, tiles. Her first tiles were decorated on her own biscuit, which she glazed and painted mainly in blue; later she turned to painting on pre-glazed commercial tiles using under-glaze colors that she fired at a high temperature, achieving excellent results. She has experimented with glass fusion, producing simple but striking designs using transparent and colored glass fused onto the surface of pre-glazed tiles. More recently, she produced a range of vividly colored glass tiles under the trade name "Lustyglaze." She produced a wide range of standard designs and also worked to commission as well as running workshops for drawing, painting, hand painted tiles, and mosaics. She retired from tile making in 2005 due to ill health.

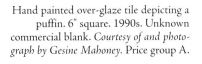

Hand painted over-glaze tile depicting a puffin. 6" square. 1990s. Unknown commercial blank. *Courtesy of and photograph by Gesine Mahoney.* Price group A.

Hand painted over-glaze tile depicting a kingfisher. 6" square. 1990s. Unknown commercial blank. *Courtesy of and photograph by Gesine Mahoney.* Price group A.

Panel of twelve hand painted over-glaze tiles depicting a peacock. Each tile 4" square. 1990s. Unknown commercial blanks. *Courtesy of and photograph by Gesine Mahoney.* Price group C (panel).

Panel of four hand painted over-glaze tiles depicting hot air balloons. Each tile 6" square. 1990s. Unknown commercial blanks. *Courtesy of and photograph by Gesine Mahoney.* Price group B (panel).

Panel of fifteen hand painted over-glaze tiles depicting a nighttime window scene. Each tile 4" square. 1990s. Unknown commercial blanks. *Courtesy of and photograph by Gesine Mahoney.* Price group C (panel).

Hand painted over-glaze tile depicting a cow. 6" square. 1990s. Unknown commercial blank. *Courtesy of and photograph by Gesine Mahoney.* Price group A.

Hand painted over-glaze tile depicting a little girl with a birthday cake. 6" square. 1990s. Unknown commercial blank. *Courtesy of and photograph by Gesine Mahoney.* Price group A.

Hand painted over-glaze tile depicting a turkey. 6" square. 1990s. Unknown commercial blank. *Courtesy of and photograph by Gesine Mahoney.* Price group A.

Hand painted over-glaze tile depicting the dish that ran away with the spoon. 6" square. 1990s. Unknown commercial blank. *Courtesy of and photograph by Gesine Mahoney.* Price group A.

Panel of six hand painted over-glaze tiles depicting a witch on her broomstick. Each tile 6" square in original frame. 1990s. Unknown commercial blanks. *Courtesy of and photograph by Gesine Mahoney.* Price group B (panel).

Panel of six hand painted over-glaze tiles depicting a sailing ship. Each tile 6" square in original frame. 1990s. Unknown commercial blanks. *Courtesy of and photograph by Gesine Mahoney.* Price group B (panel).

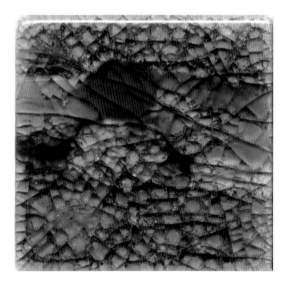

Glass fusion tile. 4" square. 1990s. Unknown commercial blank. *Courtesy of and photograph by Gesine Mahoney.* Price group A.

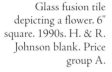

Glass fusion tile depicting a flower. 6" square. 1990s. H. & R. Johnson blank. Price group A.

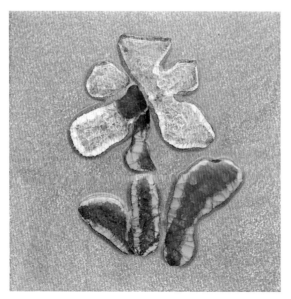

Identification and Marks

Most of Gesine Mahoney's individual tiles are unsigned, but tile panels have her signature, sometimes with the addition of "Cornwall."

Eric James Mellon 1950-

1950-1952: Earls Court, London
1952-1956: Hillesden Community, Buckinghamshire
1957- : 5 Parkfield Avenue, Bognor Regis, Sussex

Eric James Mellon was born in 1925 in Watford, Hertfordshire and joined Watford College of Art in 1939. In 1945, he started at the Central School of Art & Design, London, and in 1947 he was awarded National Diploma in Design: Illustration and became an exhibition designer for SPCK (Society for Promoting Christian Knowledge).

In 1952, he was a co-founder of the working arts community at Hillesden Vicarage in Buckinghamshire—formed to make ceramics, to paint, and to obtain design commissions. The other members of the community were John Clarke and his wife Mary, *Derek Davis* and his wife Ruth, and Martina Thomas, whom Mellon married in 1956.

At Hillesden, Eric experimented with ceramics, producing earthenwares fired at below 1100°C, decorated with colored slips, sometimes cut through to reveal the clay body. He also experimented with natural forms—flowers, bird and leaf forms, figurative work, and abstract designs—but these were not pursued later. He obtained a commission to design, make, and fit a ceramic fireplace for the consulting room of Dr. Richard Bell at Notting Hill Gate, London, which he followed with another large fireplace for the waiting room. He later undertook a bathroom depicting David and Bathsheba and a patio featuring "The Judgment of Paris" for the same patron.

About this time, Eric became absorbed by the creation of bush ash glazes for stonewares and he continues to experiment with this technique. He has developed ash glazes based on the Philadelphus bush that are able to withstand reduction firing at stoneware temperatures without acting as a flux to the oxide colors he uses. Latterly, he has specialized in images of the female nude.

Shaped hand painted tile depicting a dove. Approximately 7" wide. 1950s. *Courtesy of Eric James Mellon.* Price group C.

Large panel of shaped hand painted tiles depicting "Bathsheba." Approximately 60" x 18" overall. c.1955. *Courtesy of Eric James Mellon.* Price group G (panel).

Slabbed fireplace featuring shaped hand painted tiles depicting birds and leaves. Approximately 54" wide overall. 1956. *Courtesy of and photograph by Eric James Mellon*. Price group G (fireplace complete).

Hand painted stoneware tile with a pear ash glaze, "The Beach." 4" x 8". 1998. *Courtesy of Eric James Mellon*. Price group B.

Hand painted stoneware tile with an elm ash glaze, "Persephone." 8" x 4". 2002. Price group B.

Identification and Marks

Eric James Mellon marks his tiles on one long edge with his signature in full, a fox, the type of ash glaze used, and the date of firing.

References

Foster, Paul (editor). *Eric James Mellon, Ceramic Artist*. Otter Memorial Paper, No. 11. Chichester, Sussex: University College, 2000.

Sophie Milburn 1986-

Old Vicarage, Sibton, Suffolk

Sophie Milburn specializes in tiles on an "Egyptian paste" body, a low fired body containing soda ash. As the tile dries, so the glaze forms itself on the surface. The design is cut from a thin layer of clay colored with oxides and body stains, which is rolled into the surface of the tile. These are then fired in an electric kiln to 1010°C.

Hand decorated tile depicting a Black Headed Gull. 150mm square. 1990s. *Courtesy of Sophie Milburn*. Price group A.

Hand decorated tile depicting a Bar Tailed Godwit. 150mm square. 1990s. *Courtesy of Sophie Milburn.* Price group A.

Two hand decorated tiles depicting chickens on a copper green ground. Each tile 100mm square. 1990s. *Courtesy of Sophie Milburn.* Price group A (each).

Two hand decorated tiles depicting chickens on a cobalt blue ground. Each tile 100mm square. 1990s. *Courtesy of Sophie Milburn.* Price group A (each).

Hand decorated tile depicting a Curlew Sandpiper. 150mm square. 1990s. *Courtesy of Sophie Milburn.* Price group A.

Hand decorated tile depicting a Cyclamen. 150mm square. 1990s. *Courtesy of Sophie Milburn.* Price group A.

Identification and Marks

Painted monogram mark used on the back of plastic clay tiles.

Annabel Munn
Annabel Munn Ceramics 1990-

1990-1994: Netham Road Studios, Redfield, Bristol
1994- : Beck House, South Ambersham, Midhurst, West Sussex

Annabel Munn studied ceramics at Bristol Polytechnic, graduating in 1990. Whilst there, she was influenced by the ceramics of her tutors, Mo Jupp and Wally Keeler. She joined Netham Road Studios and initially concentrated on general ceramics, but started making tiles in 1992.

Her distinctive tiles are created by an unusual and probably unique method: she builds up layers of colored slips by painting them onto paper salvaged from Yellow Pages telephone directories. This is then applied to the wet clay tile. When the tile is leather hard, she draws and scrapes the image through the surface, exposing the layers and the bare clay beneath. The tiles are then fired in an electric kiln at between 1140°C and 1160°C. As the tiles are handmade and the nature of the manufacturing process produces variations in color and surface, no two tiles are identical and the colors also vary. Annabel produces a range of standard designs and also works to commission. In addition, she makes tiled wall hangings and sculptures from shaped tiles.

Sgraffito plastic clay tile depicting a lobster. Approximately 200mm square. 1990s. *Courtesy of Annabel Munn.* Price group B.

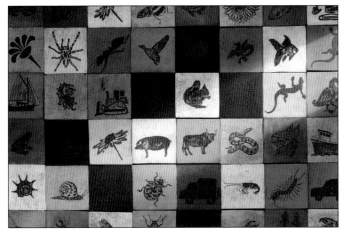

Selection of sgraffito plastic clay tiles designed as cabochons to fit plain tiles with clipped corners. Each tile 70mm square. 1990s. *Courtesy of and photograph by Annabel Munn.* Price group A (each).

Sgraffito plastic clay tile depicting an earwig. Approximately 200mm square. 1990s. *Courtesy of Annabel Munn.* Price group B.

Sgraffito plastic clay tile depicting a fish. Approximately 200mm square. 1990s. *Courtesy of Annabel Munn.* Price group B.

Sgraffito plastic clay tile depicting a heraldic eagle. Approximately 200mm square. 1990s. *Courtesy of Annabel Munn*. Price group B.

Sgraffito plastic clay tile depicting an Anomolous Tripod fish. Approximately 200mm square. 1990s. Price group B.

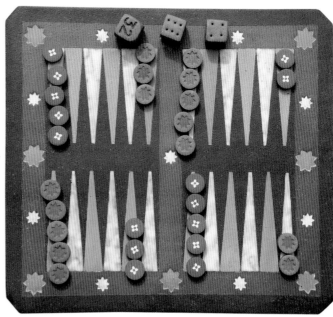

Sgraffito plastic clay backgammon tile complete with ceramic counters and dies. Approximately 225mm x 275mm. 1990s. *Courtesy of Annabel Munn.* Price group C.

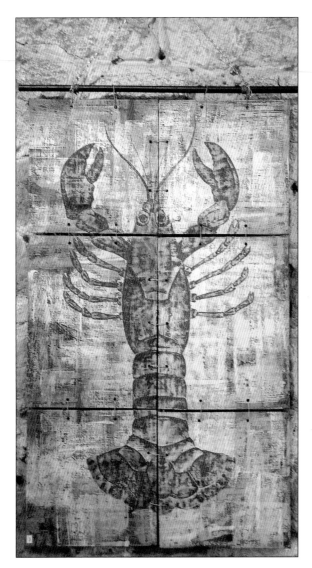

Sgraffito plastic clay wall hanging consisting of eight tiles linked with iron wire and depicting a fish. Approximately 500mm x 800mm overall. 1990s. *Courtesy of Annabel Munn.* Price group F (panel).

Identification and Marks

Painted signature mark used on the face of most tiles.

Sgraffito plastic clay wall hanging consisting of six tiles linked with iron wire and depicting a lobster. Approximately 650mm x 400mm overall. 1990s. *Courtesy of Annabel Munn.* Price group F (panel).

Two sgraffito plastic clay tile sculptures depicting a JCB digger and a Volkswagen Beetle. Each approximately 200mm wide. 1990s. *Courtesy of Annabel Munn.* Price group C (each sculpture).

William Staite Murray (b.1881-d.1962)

1919-1924: Rotherhithe, London
1924-1929: Wickham Road, Lewisham, London
1929-1939: Bray, Berkshire

Born in South East London in 1881, William Staite Murray developed an interest in painting as a teenager. In his late twenties, he attended pottery classes near his home and then went on to work at the Yeoman Pottery in Kensington, South London. In 1919, he established his own pottery in Rotherhithe, South East London, at his brother's factory premises. Here he started to work in stoneware and it is likely that this is when he commenced making tiles. His reputation as a potter grew steadily through the early 1920s and in 1925 he was appointed to the staff of the Royal College of Art, becoming Head of its Pottery Department in 1926.

He was an innovative potter and one of the first studio potters to use stoneware. His coarsely grogged body was difficult to fire and he perfected his own kiln design, which he patented. This gas-fired kiln afforded him good control and enabled the production of glazes to a consistently high quality. This was essential particularly for his pots, some of which were of quite monumental proportions. In 1929, he moved his workshop to Bray in Berkshire near the River Thames, the site of which has recently been excavated, revealing large quantities of wasters including tiles. In 1939, he retired from potting and traveled to Zimbabwe (then Rhodesia), where he found himself cut off by the Second World War. As a result, he settled there and in 1955 became a trustee of the National Arts Council of Southern Rhodesia. He died of cancer in 1962.

Four hand painted plastic clay tiles depicting fruits. Each tile 3" square. 1920s. *Courtesy of the Potteries Museum & Art Gallery, Stoke-on-Trent.* Price group C (each).

Hand painted plastic clay tile depicting a stylized tree. 6" square. 1920s. *Courtesy of the Potteries Museum & Art Gallery, Stoke-on-Trent.* Price group D.

Hand painted plastic clay tile depicting a flower. 3" square. 1920s. *Courtesy of the Potteries Museum & Art Gallery, Stoke-on-Trent.* Price group C.

Hand painted plastic clay tile depicting a stylized rose. 3" square. 1920s. *Courtesy of the Potteries Museum & Art Gallery, Stoke-on-Trent.* Price group C.

Hand painted plastic clay tile depicting plums. 3" square. 1920s. *Courtesy of the Potteries Museum & Art Gallery, Stoke-on-Trent.* Price group C.

Identification and Marks

Fragment of tile showing hexagon mark used on the face of some tiles.

Hand painted plastic clay tile depicting a stylized flower. 6½" square. 1920s. Price group D.

Distinctive backs found on 3" and 4" square tiles.

Danka Napiorkowska 1971-

1971-1982: Lustre Pottery, St Nicholas Street, Norton, Malton, North Yorkshire
1982- : Little Treforda, Trewalder, Delabole, North Cornwall

Trained at the Exeter College of Art, the Central School of Art & Design, London, and the Chelsea College of Art, London, Danka Napiorkowska first started making tiles whilst running the Lustre Pottery in North Yorkshire with Roger Michell between 1971 and 1982. Tiles were only a very small part of the output, and it is only since she moved to Cornwall in 1982 that Danka has worked principally with tiles—designing and producing panels and murals for both private and public sectors.

Danka's tiles are decorated with on-glaze enamels applied in various ways but mostly air-brushed. Initially she used British-made commercial tiles, but she now uses a wide variety from around the world, including a number of larger sized tiles used mainly for large-scale panels. After decoration, the tiles are fired in her own kilns at various temperatures dictated by the type of tile and color of enamel or luster.

Panel of hand painted over-glaze tiles depicting an exotic bird. Each tile 6" square. 1990s. Unknown commercial blanks. *Courtesy of Danka Napiorkowska, photograph by Hugh Sainsbury.* Price group B (panel).

Panel of hand painted over-glaze tiles depicting sunflowers. Each tile 100mm square. 1990s. Unknown commercial blanks. *Courtesy of Danka Napiorkowska, photograph by Hugh Sainsbury.* Price group E (complete panel).

Panel of hand painted over-glaze tiles depicting a jug of flowers. Each tile 6" square. 1990s. Unknown commercial blanks. *Courtesy of Danka Napiorkowska, photograph by Hugh Sainsbury.* Price group D (panel).

Panel of hand painted over-glaze tiles depicting an exotic bird. Each tile 6" square. 1990s. Unknown commercial blanks. *Courtesy of Danka Napiorkowska, photograph by Hugh Sainsbury.* Price group C (panel).

Identification and Marks

Although her individual tiles are not marked, Danka Napiorkowska signs her tile panels with a handwritten signature and date.

Ben Nicholson (b.1894-d.1982)

Poole Pottery 1960s

Ben Nicholson was born in 1894 in Denham, Buckinghamshire. He was a highly regarded artist of the 20th century who, during the 1920s and 1930s, specialized in landscapes and still life. His second wife was the well-known abstract sculptor, Barbara Hepworth, who influenced him towards abstract painting; he was able to create particularly evocative images with just a few simple but deft brush strokes. He is known to have painted a few tiles on *Carter and Co.* blanks in the early 1960s at *Poole Pottery.* These were glazed and fired for him by Poole Pottery. He died in 1982 in Hampstead, London.

Panel of hand painted over-glaze tiles depicting an Egyptian scene. Each tile 6" square. 1990s. Unknown commercial blanks. *Courtesy of and photograph by Danka Napiorkowska.* Price group D (panel).

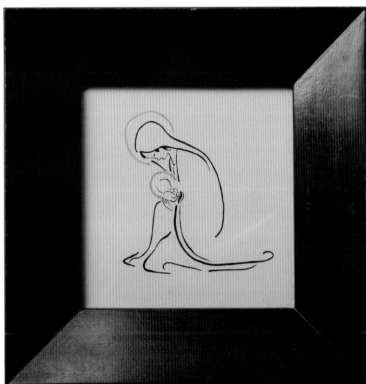

Hand painted tile depicting Madonna and Child. 6" square in original frame. Dated on reverse 17 July 1962. Carter & Co. blank. *Courtesy of Paul & Angela Pitkin.* Price group F.

Panel of hand painted over-glaze tiles depicting a scene from a saucy postcard. Each tile 100mm square. 1990s. Unknown commercial blanks. *Courtesy of and photograph by Danka Napiorkowska.* Price group F (panel).

Identification and Marks

Tiles are marked on the back with the signature "B. Nicholson" and the date.

Jan O'Highway 1979-

1979-1984: Redfield Community, Winslow, Buckinghamshire
1986-1888: Artist in Residence, New Bradwell Primary School, Milton Keynes, Buckinghamshire
1988-1990: (Traveling)
1990-2002: Studio 4, Artspace Portsmouth, 27 Brougham Road, Southsea, Hampshire
2002- : 60 The Carrions, Totnes, Devon

Jan O'Highway made her first tiles whilst studying at Brighton College of Art in the early 1960s. She had previously studied painting at Guildford College of Art but decided to go into ceramics after her time at Brighton. She also took a teacher training course with a special arts emphasis and has always had a passion for teaching ceramics, which she put to good use during her residency at New Bradwell Primary School in Milton Keynes. Whilst there, she received a community grant of £500 from the Commission for the New Towns, which en-

abled her to establish her own workshop. For a time, she worked with Mick and Sheila Casson in their pottery at Prestwood, Buckinghamshire and it was Mick Casson who encouraged her and enabled her to buy her first kiln from a mutual friend for just £10!

Although most of her work is intended for use in public spaces or private commissions, Jan does sell individual tiles as art works from exhibitions, studios, and galleries. She has also created a number of mosaic works and sometimes incorporates individual tiles into these. Her public commissions include a commemorative seat created in conjunction with blacksmith Richard Bent at Gosport in Hampshire, and a millennium way marker at Purbrook in Hampshire.

Jan's individual tiles are decorated by hand trailing or painting with earthenware glazes onto commercial biscuit sourced from *H. & R. Johnson Ltd.* and others. The tiles are fired to between 1020°C and 1060°C. Work intended for outside installation is fired onto handmade vitrified porcelain blanks or commercial quarry tiles.

Detail of a large frieze of glaze trailed, hand painted, and luster tiles, "Imaginary Forest" (tree frog). Each tile 6" square. 1980s. Unknown commercial blanks. *Courtesy of and photograph by Jan O'Highway.* Price group G (complete panel).

Detail of a large frieze of glaze trailed, hand painted and luster tiles, "Imaginary Forest" (bird of paradise). Each tile 6" square. 1980s. Unknown commercial blanks. *Courtesy of and photograph by Jan O'Highway.* Price group G (complete panel).

Glaze trailed and hand painted tile with a floral design. 6" square. c.1990. Unknown commercial blank. *Courtesy of Maggie Angus Berkowitz.* Price group A.

Detail of a panel of glaze trailed and hand painted tiles based on flip book images. Each large tile 6" square. 1990s. Unknown commercial blanks. *Courtesy of and photograph by Jan O'Highway.* Price group D (each figure panel).

Panel of forty glaze trailed and hand painted tiles, "Tree of Life." Each large tile 6" square. 1999. Unknown commercial blanks. *Courtesy of and photograph by Jan O'Highway.* Price group G (complete panel).

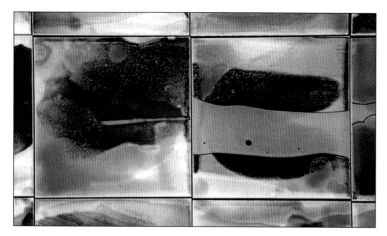

Detail of a large panel of reactive glazed and luster tiles with abstract designs. Each tile 6" square. 1990s. Unknown commercial blanks. *Courtesy of and photograph by Jan O'Highway.* Price group A (each tile).

Identification and Marks
Tiles are occasionally signed with initials "O'H."

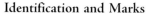

D. C. Partridge (b.1893-d.1932)

1893-1924: Ivy Lodge, Hereford, Herefordshire
1924-1932: Ham Spray House, Nr. Inkpen, Wiltshire

Dora Carrington was born at Ivy Lodge, Hereford on March 29, 1893. She was educated at Bedford High School and then attended the Slade School of Art in London from 1910-1914. In 1915, she met Vanessa Bell and Duncan Grant and became involved with the "Bloomsbury Group" and the Omega Workshops. Although she was never part of the Omega Workshops, she did paint some tiles for them on commission. In 1921, she married Ralph Partridge and adopted the name D. C. Partridge for her tile making.

In 1924, she and her husband bought Ham Spray House near Inkpen in

Wiltshire, and by 1928 she had a new studio in the grounds of the house. There she continued to paint tiles, mainly for bathrooms and fireplaces. She is said to have bought tiles "wholesale in London" and to have decorated them for sale through London shops. It appears that she did not have her own kiln but took the tiles up to London for firing. Although she produced quite a number of tiles, they were never her first love and were only made to supplement her income from painting. In July 1928, she was finding the going tough and wrote to her lover, Lytton Strachey, that, "my brain thinks of nothing but tiles." In a further letter to him in September that year, she tells him that her tiles were nautical designs, "mostly of shells, fishes and ships." She continued to paint tiles until her suicide on March 11, 1932.

Illustration from *Country Life* magazine of February 13, 1932, showing a fireplace set with Dora Carrington Partridge tiles depicting flowers and a sun. Price group G (complete fireplace).

2.—TILE PICTURE BY D. C. PARTRIDGE

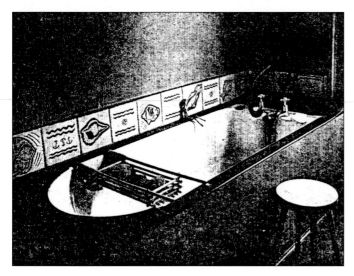

Illustration from *Design in the Home*, edited by N. Carrington, published by Country Life Ltd., London 1953, showing a bathroom set with Dora Carrington Partridge tiles depicting marine images. Price group B (each tile).

Identification and Marks
No recorded marks.

References
Gerzina, Gretchen. *A Life of Dora Carrington 1893-1932*. London: John Murray (Publishers) Ltd., 1989.

James, Philip. "Modern Fireplace Tiles." *Country Life Magazine*. February 13, 1932.

Carrington, Noël (editor). *Design in the Home*. London: Country Life Ltd., 1953.

John Pearson 1892-c.1910

Newlyn, Cornwall

John Pearson was initially employed by William de Morgan in about 1885 and whilst working on ceramic designs for de Morgan's company, he started creating hand-beaten copperware in the style of the Arts and Crafts movement. During this time, he was a founder member of the Guild of Handicraft, established in London in 1888, and became its senior metal worker. In 1892, he left de Morgan and also resigned from the Guild, going instead to Newlyn in Cornwall to instruct at the newly founded Newlyn Industrial Class under the direction of designer John Drew Mackenzie.

To complement his copper work, John Pearson decorated a small number of tiles, mainly on *Maw & Co.* blanks. These were set into trays, mirror frames, and box lids made from beaten copper. The tiles were decorated over-glaze with designs reminiscent of de Morgan but using low temperature enamels. Due to this, his tiles are quite vulnerable to wear.

Hand painted over-glaze tile depicting an eagle. 3" square. c.1905. Maw & Co. blank. Price group C.

Hand painted over-glaze tile depicting a (?)rabbit. 3" square. c.1905. Maw & Co. blank. Price group C.

Hand painted over-glaze tile depicting an owl. 3" square. c.1905. Maw & Co. blank. Price group C.

Hand painted over-glaze tile depicting a snake. 3" square. c.1905. Maw & Co. blank. Price group C.

Panel of two hand painted over-glaze tiles depicting fish. Each tile 8" square in modern frame. c.1910. Unknown commercial blanks. *Private collection*. Price group F (panel).

Identification and Marks
No recorded marks.

John Piper
Fulham Pottery 1984

184 New Kings Road, London

John Egerton Christmas Piper was born in Epsom, Surrey in 1903, the son of a wealthy solicitor. He was expected to join the family firm but wanted to pursue a career as an artist. On the death of his father in 1925, his obligation to the family business ceased and he tried to enter the Royal College of Art in South Kensington, London. Initially he was turned down, as they considered he did not have enough experience of drawing the nude. He then went to Richmond School of Art and after a year there was finally accepted into the Royal College of Art.

John Piper supplemented his income by writing art reviews and columns for magazines, as his paintings were not selling very well at that time. He was then asked to join a group of artists, "The Seven and Five," which included *Ben Nicholson*, Henry Moore, and Barbara Hepworth. During World War II, Piper joined the government War Artists scheme, painting murals for propaganda and morale boosting. For these, he was paid on an hourly basis, giving him the financial independence he craved.

In 1968, he turned to ceramics and worked with Fulham Pottery, creating large scale ceramic objects decorated in painterly fashion. His one excursion into tiles occurred in 1984, when he designed a series of four tiles depicting the seasons. These were screen printed by Fulham Pottery and produced in a limited edition of 150 sets.

Screen printed tile from the Four Seasons series. 6" square. 1984. *Courtesy of Michael Spender.* Price group C.

Identification and Marks

John Piper's tiles are signed in full on the front and have a Fulham Pottery rubber stamp mark on the back.

Bernard Rebuck
Rebuck Ceramics 1994-

5A Tasker Road, London, NW3

Bernard Rebuck has been making small runs of individual tiles as an adjunct to his other ceramic work since 1994. As he is self-taught, experimentation plays a big part in the creation of his tiles; he notes that, "I am never conscious when starting a tile, where my journey is going to end..." His designs are largely abstract and yet create curiously evocative images.

He uses standard commercial glazed tiles and powdered on-glaze enamels, usually mixed with plain water. He sometimes adds a little white sugar for stability. He uses brushes ranging from coarse Chinese to sable, but also uses fingers and fingernails on occasion to "manipulate the glazes." The tiles are fired more slowly than is normally recommended, using a 3 kilowatt electric kiln operating at 730°C - 780°C.

Hand decorated tile using finger manipulated glazes depicting a group of people. 6" square. 1990s. Unknown commercial blank. *Courtesy of and photograph by Bernard Rebuck.* Price group C.

Hand painted tile with an abstract design. 6" square. 1990s. Unknown commercial blank. *Courtesy of and photograph by Bernard Rebuck.* Price group C.

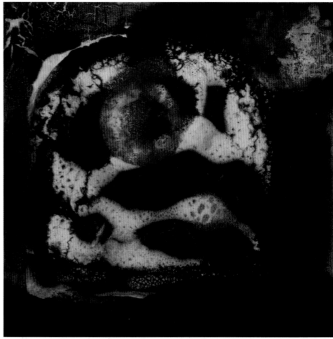

Hand painted glaze effect tile with an abstract design. 6" square. 1990s. Unknown commercial blank. *Courtesy of and photograph by Bernard Rebuck.* Price group C.

Hand painted tile with an abstract portrait. 6" square. 1990s. Unknown commercial blank. *Courtesy of and photograph by Bernard Rebuck.* Price group C.

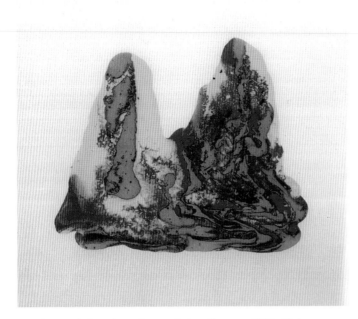

Hand painted tile with an abstract design. 6" square. 1990s. Unknown commercial blank. *Courtesy of and photograph by Bernard Rebuck.* Price group C.

Hand painted tile with an abstract design. 6" square. 1990s. Unknown commercial blank. *Courtesy of and photograph by Bernard Rebuck.* Price group C.

Hand painted tile with an abstract design. 6" square. 1990s. Unknown commercial blank. *Courtesy of and photograph by Bernard Rebuck.* Price group C.

Hand painted tile with an abstract cityscape. 8" square. 1990s. Unknown commercial blank. *Courtesy of and photograph by Bernard Rebuck.* Price group C.

Hand painted tile with an abstract landscape. 6" x 8". 1990s. Unknown commercial blank. *Courtesy of and photograph by Bernard Rebuck.* Price group C.

Identification and Marks

Initial "R" mark found on the face of most tiles.

John Reilly
The Ventnor Pottery Studio c.1958-1985

Victoria Street, Ventnor, Isle of Wight

John Reilly studied at Kingston-on-Thames Art College from 1949-1952 before moving to the Isle of Wight in 1954. For a number of years he worked in partnership with another potter, *Jo Lester*, at Niton. In about 1958, he established his own pottery in Ventnor. His main output was a series of rectangular, circular and oval slip-cast plaques, which he decorated with a wide variety of designs. He also decorated commercial biscuit tiles purchased from *Richards Tiles Ltd.* and *Carter & Co.* of Poole. Many of these were sold in whitewood frames in which the tile could be placed either flush or recessed.

Although his techniques varied over the years, most of his tiles were hand painted in colored glazes on the white body and fired to 1100°C. His designs included animal caricatures and also some splendid abstract work. He also experimented with unusual glazes in an attempt to create the effect of an oil painting on tiles. A number of his tile panels were made up into tabletops or framed.

Since 1981, John Reilly has concentrated increasingly on his painting and eventually ceased tile making in 1985.

Hand painted tile with a floral design. 6" square. 1963. Carter & Co. blank. *Courtesy of Mary Bentley.* Price group B.

Four hand painted glaze effect tiles with abstract designs. Each tile 3" square. 1960s. Richards Tiles blanks. *Courtesy of John Reilly.* Price group B (each).

Panel of twenty hand painted tiles with an abstract design. Large tiles 6" square set in original wrought iron table top. c.1960. Unknown commercial floor tile blanks. *Courtesy of John Reilly*. Price group F (table complete).

Panel of eight hand painted and wax resist tiles with an abstract design. Each tile 6" square set in original wooden table top. c.1960. Unknown commercial blanks. *Courtesy of John Reilly*. Price group F (table complete).

Panel of six hand painted tiles with an abstract design utilizing an experimental sodium silicate glaze. Each tile 6" square. 1960s. Unknown commercial blanks. *Courtesy of John Reilly.* Price group E (panel).

Hand painted tile depicting a lady out walking. 6" square. 1960s. *Courtesy of John Reilly.* Price group C.

Hand painted glaze effect tile depicting "Home." 13" x 14". 1960s. *Courtesy of John Reilly.* Price group E.

Panel of twelve hand painted glaze effect and wax resist tiles depicting Noah's Ark. Each tile 6" square. 1960s. Unknown commercial blanks. *Courtesy of John Reilly.* Price group F (panel).

Panel of six hand painted glaze effect and wax resist tiles depicting a galleon. Each tile 6" square. 1960s. Unknown commercial blanks. *Courtesy of John Reilly.* Price group E (panel).

Four sgraffito tiles depicting animals. Each tile 3" square. 1960s. Richards Tiles blanks. *Courtesy of John Reilly.* Price group B (each).

Hand painted tile depicting a flower. 6" square. c.1970. Pilkington's + Carter blank. *Courtesy of John Reilly.* Price group B.

Hand painted tile depicting a cat. 4¼" square in original wooden frame. 1964.
Richards Tiles blank. Price group B.

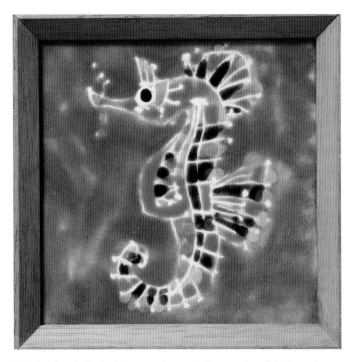

Hand painted tile depicting a lion. 4¼" square in original wooden frame.
1968. Carter & Co. blank. Price group B.

Hand painted tile depicting a seahorse. 4¼" square in original wooden
frame. 1964. Richards Tiles blank. *Courtesy of Roger Hensman.* Price
group B.

Hand painted tile depicting a dragon. 6″ square. c.1970. Candy & Co. blank. Price group B.

Hand painted tile depicting a seahorse. 6″ square. c.1970. Candy & Co. blank. Price group B.

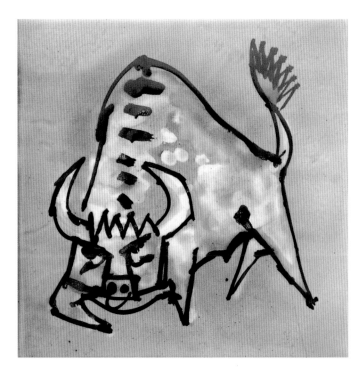

Hand painted tile depicting a bull. 6″ square. c.1970. Candy & Co. blank. Price group B.

Hand painted tile depicting a lion. 6″ square. c.1970. Candy & Co. blank. Price group B.

Rubber stamp mark on Carter & Co. 4¼" blank.

R Ventnor.

Signature mark used on some tile panels and plaques.

Occasionally, tiles were signed "J Reilly" or had "The Ventnor Pottery Studio" hand painted on the back.

Rosemary Robus
Robus Ceramics 1980-

1980-1990: Ladwood Acrise, Folkestone, Kent
1990- : Evington Park, Hastingleigh, Ashford, Kent

Rosemary Robus was initially inspired by traditional delftware tiles, which she has reproduced and elaborated upon for over twenty years. Painted in the traditional technique of oxide colors in a tin-glaze, her range includes polychrome as well as blue and white tiles. In more recent years, her business has branched out into handmade floor tiles, sometimes with textured glazed terra cotta inserts, and large-scale terra cotta statuary, path edgings, and architectural details. The company has also recreated the traditional Kentish mathematical tiles used originally to clad and update medieval buildings in the Georgian style.

Employing a staff of five, the company makes all its own tiles, which are hand pressed from wooden molds and glazed by hand.

Three hand painted tin glaze tiles with traditional delftware designs. Each tile 5" square. 1990s. _Courtesy of and photograph by Rosemary Robus_. Price group A (each).

Two hand painted tin glaze tiles with floral designs. Each tile 3" square. 1990s. _Courtesy of and photograph by Rosemary Robus_. Price group A (each).

Two hand painted tin glaze tiles from a larger panel, with traditional early delftware designs. Each tile 5" square. 1990s. *Courtesy of and photograph by Rosemary Robus.* Price group A (each).

Panel of thirty-six hand painted tin glaze tiles, "Medieval Animals." Each tile 5" square. 1990s. *Courtesy of and photograph by Rosemary Robus.* Price group F (panel).

Identification and Marks
No identifying marks.

Elisabeth Roussel 1969-c.1994

26 High Street, Woodstock, Oxfordshire

Elisabeth Roussel specialized in hand painted floral and animal tiles. For exterior use, these were painted onto black bodied stoneware floor tiles purchased from Belgian and German manufacturers. Her interior tiles were painted on *Pilkington's Tiles Ltd.* blanks.

Her technique was to apply a thin white glaze to the biscuit. This was then sprayed with background colors that were scraped away to create the design (sgraffito). Other glazes were then applied to complete the design. Firing took place in an oxidizing atmosphere at 1040°C.

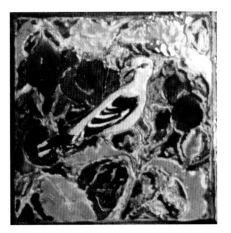

Hand painted stoneware tile depicting a bird. 6" square. 1980s. *Courtesy of and photograph by Elisabeth Roussel.* Price group B.

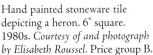

Hand painted and impressed stoneware tile depicting a flower and butterflies. 6" square. 1980s. *Courtesy of and photograph by Elisabeth Roussel.* Price group B.

Hand painted stoneware tile depicting a heron. 6" square. 1980s. *Courtesy of and photograph by Elisabeth Roussel.* Price group B.

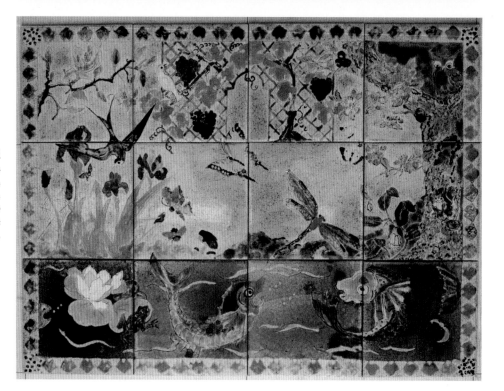

Panel of twelve hand painted stoneware tiles depicting a pond scene. Each tile 6" square. 1980s. *Courtesy of and photograph by Elisabeth Roussel.* Price group E (panel).

Hand painted tile depicting cornflowers. 6" square. 1980s. *Courtesy of and photograph by Elisabeth Roussel.* Price group B.

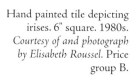

Hand painted stoneware tile depicting a dragon. 6" square. 1980s. *Courtesy of and photograph by Elisabeth Roussel.* Price group B.

Hand painted tile depicting irises. 6" square. 1980s. *Courtesy of and photograph by Elisabeth Roussel.* Price group B.

Identification and Marks

Her tiles are usually signed ER , occasionally EB.

Initials mark used on front of most tiles.

Initials mark used occasionally on front of tiles.

Christopher Russell c.1964-c.1980

c.1953-c.1970: The Studio, High Street, Swanage, Dorset
   (1957-c.1960: Barbados)
c.1970-c.2000: West Holme House, near Wareham, Dorset

Christopher Russell was born of a Russian mother in about 1933. His father taught at Weymouth Art School and painted inn signs for a living. Christopher established his first pottery in the High Street, Swanage in the early 1950s, producing pots with abstract and modernist designs that were also sold by Heals in London and other outlets.

In 1957, Christopher took a holiday in Barbados and there discovered a small, rural pottery industry, which he was asked to take under his wing by Wolf Mankowitz, who was then British Council Representative to the island. Christopher stayed for a few years before returning to Britain, where he started to make tiles as well as pots, including a number of prestigious commissions for Madame Prunier's Fish Restaurant in St. James's, London. A tile panel that was surplus to this project is shown here. Christopher also designed and made tiles to cover a large circular column for the Library at Swanage, opened on October 18, 1965 (still in situ), and several large panels for a local convent/school (now removed). Another local hotel, the Knoll House at Studland, also has a number of tiles, panels, and even tiled coat hooks still in existence, all designed and made by Christopher Russell.

Christopher used a combination of techniques, including wax resist, modeling, hand painting, and glass fusion. He sourced his colored glasses from nearby Buckfast Abbey as offcuts from their stained glass studio. He seems to have used blanks bought in from *Carter and Co.* and possibly other commercial tile manufacturers. In the 1970s, Christopher made less and less tiles and stopped altogether in about 1980, turning his talent to writing and presenting short radio programs. He is thought to have moved to Thailand in the 1990s, but all efforts to locate his current whereabouts have failed.

Hand painted wax resist and glass fusion tile with a stylized flower design. 6" square. 1964. Carter & Co. blank. *Courtesy of Roger Hensman.* Price group A.

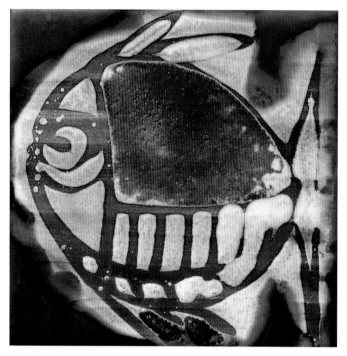

Hand painted wax resist and glass fusion tile with a stylized fish design. 6" square. 1966. Carter & Co. blank. *Courtesy of Roger Hensman.* Price group B.

Hand painted wax resist and glass fusion tile with a stylized flower design. 6" square. 1968. Carter & Co. blank. Price group A.

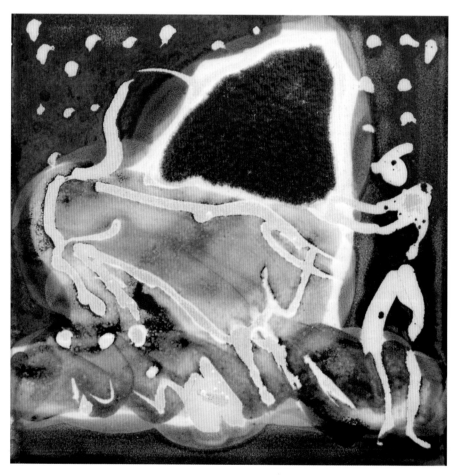

Hand painted wax resist and glass fusion tile depicting a bullfighter. 6" square. 1965. Carter & Co. blank. *Courtesy of Angela Sherborne.* Price group B.

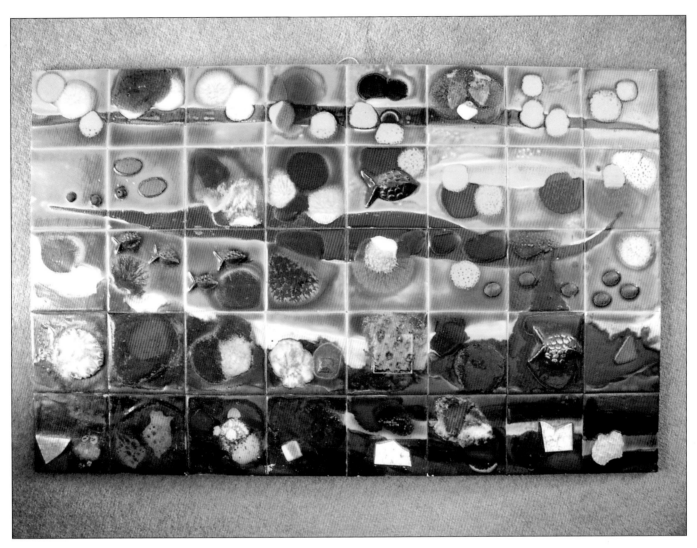

Panel of forty hand painted, wax resist, glass fusion and raised modeled tiles depicting an underwater scene. Each tile 4¼" square. c.1964. Unknown commercial blanks. This panel was a surplus one from the decoration of Madame Prunier's Fish Restaurant, St. James's Street, London and was presented by the artist to Angela Sherborne in the early 1970s. *Courtesy of Angela Sherborne.* Price group E (panel).

Another view of the panel of 416 hand painted, wax resist, glass fusion and raised modeled tiles depicting birds in flight. Each tile 6" x 3". 1965. Unknown commercial blanks. Swanage Library. *Courtesy of Dorset County Council Library Service.*

Part of a panel of 416 hand painted, wax resist, glass fusion and raised modeled tiles depicting birds in flight. Each tile 6" x 3". 1965. Unknown commercial blanks. Made for the Public Library, Swanage, Dorset. *Courtesy of Dorset County Council Library Service.* No price group (site-specific).

A detail from the Swanage Library Panel.

Panel of forty-five hand painted, wax resist, glass fusion and raised modeled tiles depicting Kings and Queens. Each tile 6" square. c.1964. Unknown commercial blanks. Knoll House Hotel, Studland, Dorset. *Courtesy of Knoll House Hotel.* Price group E (panel).

Panel of twenty-one hand painted, wax resist, glass fusion and raised modeled tiles depicting a cock and a hen. Each large tile 6" square. c.1964. Unknown commercial blanks. Knoll House Hotel. *Courtesy of Knoll House Hotel.* Price group E (panel).

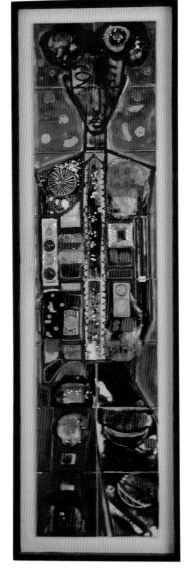

Panel of sixteen hand painted, wax resist, glass fusion and raised modeled tiles depicting a female figure. Each tile 6" square. c.1964. Unknown commercial blanks. Knoll House Hotel. *Courtesy of Knoll House Hotel.* Price group E (panel).

Panel of nine relief molded plastic clay tiles depicting a sunburst. Centre tile approximately 12" diameter. c.1964. One of three similar panels around the swimming pool at the Knoll House Hotel. *Courtesy of Knoll House Hotel.* No price group (site-specific).

Panel of mosaic made from pot shards depicting an eagle. Wingspan approximately 24". c.1964. One of three similar panels around the swimming pool at Knoll House Hotel, Studland, Dorset. The shards appear to have been wasters and/ or trial pieces *Courtesy of Knoll House Hotel.* No price group (site-specific).

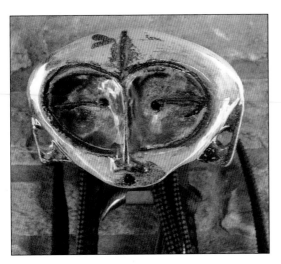

Plastic clay coat hook in the form of a face. Approximately 5" across. c.1964. One of two from the Manager's Office at the Knoll House Hotel. *Courtesy of Knoll House Hotel.* No price group (site-specific).

Identification and Marks

Hand painted mark on Carter & Co. 6" square blank. c.1965-1970. This tile has a Carter date mark for 1968.

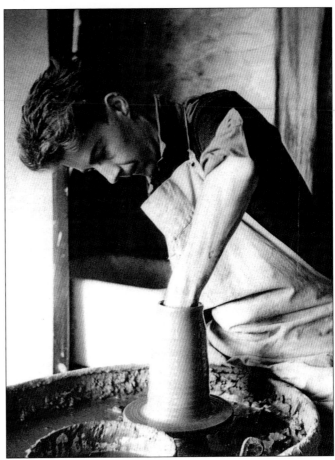

A photograph of Christopher Russell at the wheel, c.1960. *Courtesy of Angela Sherborne.*

Jill Salaman 1929-1950

Selsey, Sussex

Jill Salaman was a craft potter working at Selsey in Sussex from 1929 to 1950. In addition to pots, she also produced a small range of tin-glazed tiles during the 1930s and possibly for a short time after World War II. These were produced on the same heavily grogged earthenware body that she used for her pots.

Hand painted tile, "Danse Macabre." 5" square. 1930s. Price group C.

Hand painted tile depicting a horse rider. 5" square. 1930s. Price group C.

Identification and Marks

Tiles are also marked with a painted signature "Jill S" on the front.

Impressed mark used on plastic clay tiles.

David & Louise Salsbury 1997-

1997-2003: 231 Cossington Road, Sileby, Leicestershire
2003- : 39 Sidford High Street, Sidford, Sidmouth, Devon

David and Louise Salsbury produce individually decorated pots, tiles, and tile panels depicting animals and local scenes, plus press-molded tiles using real leaves pressed into the clay. A slab roller and various sizes of tile cutter are used to form the tile body, as well as cutting larger slabs by hand. They use Earthstone hand building clay or a similar white, grogged body that they biscuit fire and decorate with under-glaze colors and oxides using soft haired brushes and sponging. David Salsbury produces the hand painted tiles and Louise Salsbury makes the tiles impressed with natural leaves.

A few of their larger tile panels have been decorated on *H. & R. Johnson Ltd.* or *H. & E. Smith Ltd.* commercial biscuit. A transparent earthenware glaze is applied over the decoration and glost fired.

Hand painted tile by David Salsbury, depicting a beehive. Approx. 5¼" square in original wooden frame. 1990s. *Courtesy of and photograph by David & Louise Salsbury.* Price group B.

Hand painted tile by David Salsbury, depicting the beach at Beer in Devon. Approx. 5¼" square in original wooden frame. 1990s. *Courtesy of and photograph by David & Louise Salsbury.* Price group B.

Hand painted tile by David Salsbury, depicting a sailing boat. Approx. 2" square in original wooden frame. 1990s. *Courtesy of and photograph by David & Louise Salsbury.* Price group A.

Hand painted tile by David Salsbury, depicting a crab. Approx. 5¼" square in original wooden frame. 1990s. *Courtesy of and photograph by David & Louise Salsbury.* Price group B.

Hand painted tile by David Salsbury, depicting geese. Approx. 5¼" square in original wooden frame. 1990s. *Courtesy of and photograph by David & Louise Salsbury.* Price group B.

Hand painted tile by David Salsbury, depicting pigs. Approx. 5¼" square in original wooden frame. 1990s. *Courtesy of and photograph by David & Louise Salsbury.* Price group B.

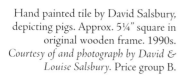

Hand painted tile by David Salsbury, depicting Saddleback pigs. Approx. 5¼" square in original wooden frame. 1990s. *Courtesy of and photograph by David & Louise Salsbury.* Price group B.

Panel of four hand painted tiles by David Salsbury, depicting a rockpool. Each tile approx. 5¼" square in original wooden frame. 1990s. *Courtesy of and photograph by David & Louise Salsbury.* Price group D (panel).

Hand painted tile by David Salsbury, depicting a robin. Approx. 2" square in original wooden frame. 1990s. *Courtesy of and photograph by David & Louise Salsbury.* Price group A.

Hand painted tile by David Salsbury, depicting a seahorse. Approx. 5¼"
square in original wooden frame. 1990s. *Courtesy of and photograph by
David & Louise Salsbury.* Price group B.

Panel of two hand painted tiles by David Salsbury, depicting "West from Salcombe Hill Cliff," signed on back "David & Louise
Salsbury." Each tile approx. 5¼" square in original wooden frame. 1990s. Price group C (panel).

Impressed and hand painted tile by Louise
Salsbury, depicting a horse-chestnut leaf.
Approx. 5¼" square in original wooden
frame. 1990s. *Courtesy of and photograph by
David & Louise Salsbury.* Price group B.

Impressed and hand painted
tile by Louise Salsbury,
depicting twin oak leaves.
Approx. 8" x 6" in original
wooden frame. 1990s.
*Courtesy of and photograph by
David & Louise Salsbury.*
Price group B.

A selection of work in progress, 2" hand painted tiles.

Hand painted tile by David Salsbury, depicting a sheep. Approx. 5¼" square in original wooden frame. 1990s. *Courtesy of and photograph by David & Louise Salsbury.* Price group B.

Identification and Marks

David and Louise Salsbury use their painted initials "D & LS" or "L & DS" on the front of individual tiles. They also sign larger panels in full.

Paul Scott
Cumbrian Blue(s) 1972-

Holly Cottage, Blencogo, Wilton, Cumbria

Paul Scott has been fascinated with the techniques of printing onto ceramics since the early 1970s when he studied at St. Martin's College, Lancaster. His work over the years has progressed from printing with reactive glazes onto commercial unglazed biscuit to his current production involving under-glaze printing and hand coloring on porcelain. Most of his work has been produced to commission and his projects have included porcelain wall panels for the main entrance of Queen Elizabeth Hospital, Gateshead (1994) and three panels for the Ophthalmic Services reception area of the Royal Victoria Infirmary, Newcastle (1998).

Paul has abandoned the regular rectangular shape of conventional tiles in favor of using irregular interlocking shapes that follow the contours of the design, somewhat akin to the mosaic technique *opus sectile*. He has also written extensively on the subject of ceramics and print, and was the Norma Lipman research fellow at the University of Newcastle upon Tyne from 1999-2001. He is a director of the Artists Information Company and a member of the International Academy of Ceramics. He regularly lectures and runs workshops in Europe and North America, and his work has been featured in exhibitions worldwide.

Opus sectile panel of hand painted porcelain tiles entitled "Hills, Hospitals and Things." Overall size approximately 800mm x 1300mm. 1994. *Courtesy of and photograph by Paul Scott.* Price group G (panel).

Three hand painted porcelain tiles entitled "Landscape Arrows." Various sizes. 1995. *Courtesy of and photograph by Paul Scott.* Price group B (each).

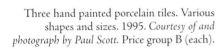Three hand painted porcelain tiles. Various shapes and sizes. 1995. *Courtesy of and photograph by Paul Scott.* Price group B (each).

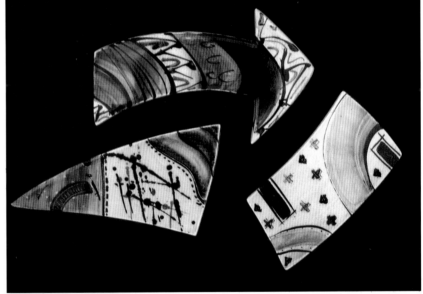

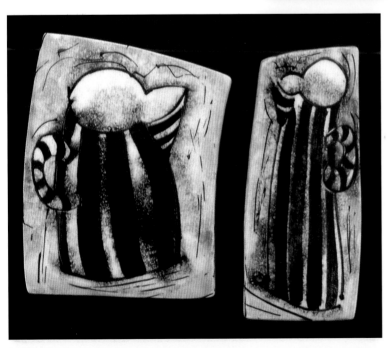

Two hand painted porcelain tiles entitled "Jugs." Various sizes. 1995. *Courtesy of and photograph by Paul Scott.* Price group B (each).

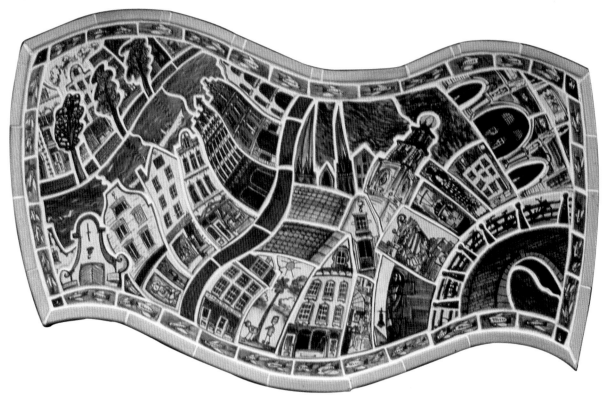

Opus sectile panel of hand painted porcelain tiles entitled "The Scott Collection: Amsterdam in Cumbrian Blue." Overall size approximately 660mm x 1090mm. 1996. *Courtesy of and photograph by Paul Scott*. Price group G (panel).

Detail of "The Scott Collection: Amsterdam in Cumbrian Blue." *Courtesy of and photograph by Paul Scott*.

Detail of a panel of hand painted and decal printed tiles entitled "Abstracting Landscape (Brieselang)." Overall size of panel 200mm x 1500mm. 1997. *Courtesy of and photograph by Paul Scott.*

Detail of a panel of hand painted and decal printed tiles entitled "Abstracting Landscape (Brieselang)." Overall size of panel 200mm x 1500mm. 1997. *Courtesy of and photograph by Paul Scott.*

Hand printed tile depicting a statue. 150mm square. 1997. Argentine blank. *Courtesy of Maggie Angus Berkowitz.* Price group B.

Fire screen set with opus sectile panels of hand painted and decal printed porcelain tiles. Overall size approximately 1000mm x 2000mm. 1997. *Courtesy of and photograph by Paul Scott.* Price group G (fire screen complete)

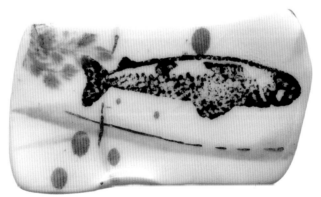

Hand painted and decal printed miniature porcelain tile depicting a fish. Approximately 25mm x 50mm. 1999. Price group A.

Identification and Marks

Paul Scott uses a variety of painted and printed marks on the backs of his tiles, featuring his name or "Cumbrian Blue(s)."

References

Scott, Paul & Bennett, Terry. *Hot Off the Press: Ceramics in Print*. London: Bellew Publishing Co. Ltd., 1996.

Scott, Paul. *Painted Clay: Graphic Arts and the Ceramic Surface*. London: A. & C. Black (Publishers) Ltd., 2001.

Scott, Paul. *Ceramics and Print*. London: A. & C. Black (Publishers) Ltd., 2nd edition, 2002.

Exhibition Catalogue. *Paul Scott Cumbrian Blue(s)*. Carlisle: Tullie House Museum & Art Gallery, 2003.

Kitty Shepherd 1992-

1992-2003: Amberley Museum Pottery, Amberley, Sussex
2003- : The Mill Studio, Ford Lane, Arundel, Sussex

Kitty Shepherd's fascination for pottery began as a child; at the age of five, she was, as she puts it, "a ditch dweller and den builder." As she dug, she uncovered many shards of pottery, including blue and white wares and also some slipwares. Her collection grew and in 1977 she began to work on a number of archeological digs in and around Chichester, where she was studying for her G.C.S.E. "A" levels in Art, Ceramics, and Drama. At college, she had an inspired teacher whose enthusiasm rekindled her love of pottery—in particular, slipware.

She eventually indulged this passion when she started as resident potter at Amberley Museum in 1992. She has had a number of successful exhibitions and continues to work creating slip-trailed and sgraffito pots and tiles.

Sgraffito tile entitled "Clockwork Fish." Approximately 10" x 12" in original maple frame. 2002. *Courtesy of Kitty Shepherd*. Price group B.

Slip trailed and hand painted tile entitled "B52." Approximately 10" x 8" in original maple frame. 2004. *Courtesy of Kitty Shepherd*. Price group B.

Slip trailed and hand painted tile entitled "Double Dyson." Approximately 8" x 6" in original maple frame. 2004. *Courtesy of Kitty Shepherd*. Price group B.

Slip trailed and hand painted tile entitled "Lemon Tree." Approximately 8" x 10" in original maple frame. 2004. *Courtesy of Kitty Shepherd.* Price group C.

Identification and Marks

Kitty Shepherd signs most of her tiles on the back in full or with initials, together with the date.

Clive Simmonds (b.1938-d.1997)
Intaglio Designs 1963-1978

1963-1978: 5 White Hart Street, Thetford, Norfolk; and Lavenham, Norfolk
1978-c.1985: South Australia

Born in 1938, Clive O'Brien Simmonds was educated at Wymondham College, Norwich School of Art, and Bournemouth College of Art, where he gained a National Diploma in Graphic Design. After leaving college, he taught for a while at a number of schools in East Anglia before setting up Intaglio Designs with his wife, Margaret Frances Simmonds, in 1963, eventually becoming a limited company on May 4, 1967.

Clive specialized in a large range of one-off special designs mainly based on a circular motif, incorporating up to four tones of red and orange set against a background of black, purple, or brown. The technique involved drawing the design onto the surface of a commercial biscuit tile using a wax resist. The tile was then dipped in the background color glaze and fired to 1000°C. The areas left clear by the wax resist were then filled with layers of different color high-flux glazes made to Clive's own recipes and re-fired at 1150°C. The orange and red glazes used were cadmium-based. In addition to these individual abstract tiles, Clive produced a number of larger tile panels and single tiles featuring owls and other motifs. Nineteen of the company's designs were selected for the Design Centres in London and Glasgow and their work was also exhibited at a number of galleries around the country. Biscuit tiles were sourced from *Hereford Tiles Ltd.* and *H. & R. Johnson Ltd.*

In 1978, Clive and Margaret emigrated to Australia where they continued to produce similar tiles until the mid 1980s, when the demand for such designs dropped off. Clive then diversified into making high quality pierced and slip-decorated pottery. In the late 1980s, Clive gave up pottery to work in the wine industry and eventually became manager of Noon's Winery in South Australia. In 1996, he was diagnosed with colon cancer and died in October 1997.

Hand painted wax resist glaze effect tile with an abstract design. 6" square in modern frame. c.1968. Hereford Tiles blank. *Courtesy of Paul & Angela Pitkin.* Price group B.

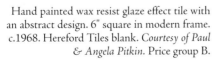

Hand painted wax resist glaze effect tile with an abstract design. 6" square in modern frame. c.1968. Hereford Tiles blank. *Courtesy of Paul & Angela Pitkin.* Price group B.

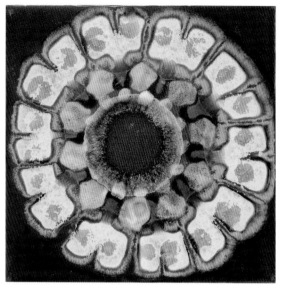

Hand painted wax resist glaze effect tile with an abstract design. 6″ square. c.1970. Hereford Tiles blank. *Courtesy of Zena Corrigan.* Price group B.

Panel of six hand painted wax resist glaze effect tiles depicting an owl. Each tile 6″ square. c.1968. Unknown commercial blanks. *Courtesy of and photograph by Margaret Simmonds.* Price group E (panel).

Hand painted wax resist glaze effect tile depicting an owl. 4¼″ square. c.1970. Hereford Tiles blank. Price group B.

Hand painted wax resist glaze effect tile with an abstract design. 6"
diameter. 1977. H. & R. Johnson blank. Price group B.

Photograph of Clive Simmonds in his studio, surrounded by examples of
his tiles. *Photograph courtesy of Margaret Simmonds.*

Photograph of wall in Clive Simmonds studio showing range of glaze effect tiles. *Photograph courtesy of Margaret Simmonds.*

Identification and Marks

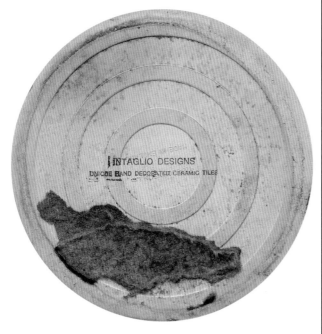

Rubber stamp mark, seen here on H. & R. Johnson 6" diameter blank.

Hand painted and sgraffito tile depicting two fish. 6" square. 2002. H. & E. Smith blank. *Courtesy of Penny Simpson.* Price group B.

Penny Simpson 1980-

42 Court Street, Moretonhampstead, Devon

Penny Simpson graduated from the University of Essex with a degree in English Literature, but was attracted to making pottery and in 1980 established her workshop at Moretonhampstead in Devon. In addition to pots made in red earthenware clay and decorated with colored slips, she also decorates commercial tile blanks sourced from *H. & R. Johnson Ltd.* These are made using a similar technique to her pots, employing sgraffito decoration and taking their inspiration from nature. From 1980 to 1999, she organized occasional day workshops and pottery classes for children, mostly of primary school age both in school and at her workshop. She has also run classes for adults in pottery and tile making.

Hand painted and sgraffito tile depicting a bird. 6" square. 1988. H. & R. Johnson blank. *Courtesy of Roger Hensman.* Price group B.

Hand painted and sgraffito tile depicting a fish. 6" square. 2002. H. & E. Smith blank. *Courtesy of Penny Simpson.* Price group B.

Hand painted and sgraffito tile depicting a dragonfly. 6" square. 2002. H. & E. Smith blank. Price group B.

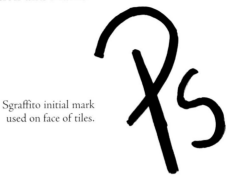

Carol Sinclair
Carol Sinclair Ceramics 1991-
Sinclair Wilson 2000-

1991- : 10 Westcroft Court, Kirkton, Livingston, near Edinburgh, Scotland (Home and Studio)
1991- : Unit 3 Albion Business Centre, 78 Albion Road, Edinburgh (Studio)
2000-2003: Cannongate Edinburgh (Showroom)

Carol Sinclair started making tiles in 1991, having studied for a degree in ceramics at Grey's School of Art, Aberdeen. She had worked in other ceramic fields but decided to concentrate on tiles following a period with *Fired Earth*, which showed her the potential of handmade tiles. Her first tiles were hand painted with marine subjects and animals and included an unusual range of hand-marbled tiles. She now concentrates on handmade, freehand cut, and molded high-fired earthenware tiles produced from hand carved plaster molds. These are decorated with slip, oxides, and glazes.

Carol has worked with a number of different part-time artists and designers, including Ceri White (who now manages their studio) and Fiona McIntosh.

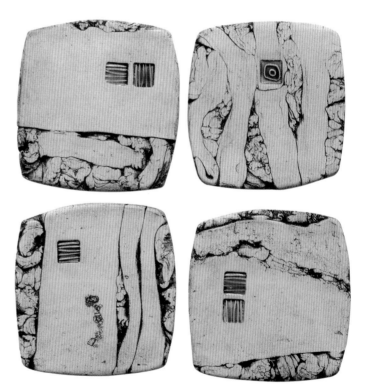

Four press molded and partly glazed high fired plastic clay earthenware tiles from the "Flintstone" range. Each tile approximately 100mm square. c.2000. *Courtesy of Carol Sinclair.* Price group A (each).

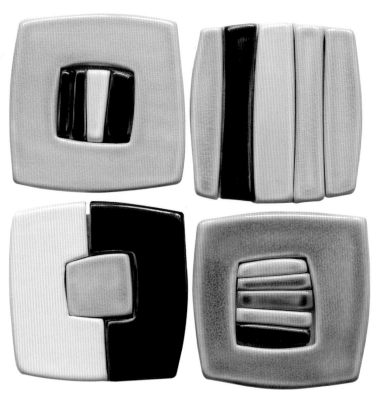

Four hand cut and glazed high fired earthenware multi-part tiles from the "Flintstone" range. Each tile approximately 100mm square. c.2000. *Courtesy of Carol Sinclair.* Price group A (each).

Hand marbled tile. 6" square. c.2000. H. & R. Johnson blank. The technique used to decorate this tile is identical to the historic method of producing hand marbled paper. *Courtesy of Carol Sinclair.* Price group A.

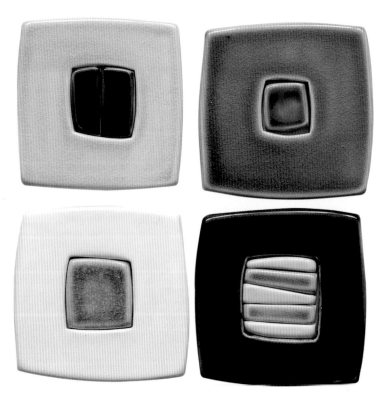

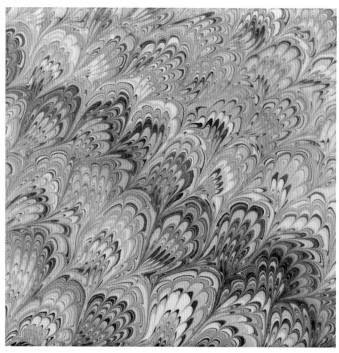

Four hand cut and glazed high fired earthenware multi-part tiles from the "Flintstone" range. Each tile approximately 100mm square. c.2000. *Courtesy of Carol Sinclair.* Price group A (each).

Hand marbled tile. 6" square. c.2000. H. & R. Johnson blank. The technique used to decorate this tile is identical to the historic method of producing hand marbled paper. *Courtesy of Carol Sinclair.* Price group A.

Two press molded stained high fired plastic clay earthenware tiles from the "Pictish" range. Each tile approximately 80mm square. c.2000. *Courtesy of Carol Sinclair.* Price group A (each)

Press molded stained high fired plastic clay earthenware tile from the "Pictish" range. 160mm square. c.2000. *Courtesy of Carol Sinclair.* Price group A.

Press molded stained high fired plastic clay earthenware tile from the "Pictish" range. 160mm square. c.2000. *Courtesy of Carol Sinclair.* Price group A.

Press molded stained high fired plastic clay earthenware tile from the "Pictish" range. 160mm square. c.2000. *Courtesy of Carol Sinclair.* Price group A.

Impressed mark used on the back of plastic clay stoneware tiles.

Janet Steele
Norton Tile Co. Ltd. 1995-

The Coach House, Norton Lane, Norton, Nr Chichester, West Sussex

Janet Steele established Norton Tile Company as a small cottage-craft business in 1995 and specializes in designing, hand-making, and painting tiles, mainly to commission. She says, "I have always painted, a sort of malady if you like; blank bits of paper drive me mad and white walls offer an irresistible canvas. I came to ceramics after a dear uncle sadly died of cancer and left me enough money to purchase a kiln. His desire to see me 'make money' out of a natural gift he said."

Janet works in a wide variety of techniques, including tube-lining, hand painting, relief molding, and screen printing. Although her work is mainly to commission she does have standard designs that she will repeat to order. She makes most of her tiles herself, but sometimes uses biscuit tiles supplied by *Clayworth Potteries.* Firing is by electric kiln and mostly at earthenware temperatures.

Janet is also involved in a certain amount of reproduction and restoration work, often small scale but very specialized. She has reproduced a number of transfer printed and tube-lined Victorian designs.

Panel of thirteen hand painted alkaline glazed plastic clay tiles recreating an early Abbasid tile panel, painted by Janet Steele. Each star tile approximately 6" diameter. 1990s. *Courtesy of Janet Steele.* Price group D (panel).

Panel of eight hand painted tiles with a repeating Art Nouveau design, "Columbine," designed and painted by Janet Steele. Each large tile 150mm square. 1990s. *Courtesy of Janet Steele.* Price group E (panel).

Panel of sixteen hand painted plastic clay tiles depicting apples, designed and painted by Janet Steele. Each tile 100mm square. 1990s. *Courtesy of Janet Steele.* Price group D (panel).

Hand painted plastic clay tile with a design from the "Courses of a Meal" series, designed and painted by Janet Steele. 150mm square. 1990s. *Courtesy of Janet Steele.* Price group A.

Hand painted plastic clay tile with a design from the "Cupcakes" series, designed and painted by Janet Steele. 150mm square. 1990s. *Courtesy of Janet Steele.* Price group A.

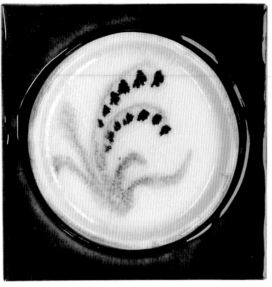

Two relief molded and hand painted plastic clay tiles depicting bluebells, designed and painted by Janet Steele. Each tile approximately 100mm square. 1990s. *Courtesy of Janet Steele.* Price group A (each).

Hand painted plastic clay tile with a design from the "Shoes" series, designed and painted by Janet Steele. 150mm square. 1990s. *Courtesy of Janet Steele.* Price group A.

Two hand painted plastic clay tiles with designs from the "Delft Style Birds and Flowers" series, designed and painted by Janet Steele. Each tile 100mm square. 1990s. *Courtesy of Janet Steele.* Price group A (each).

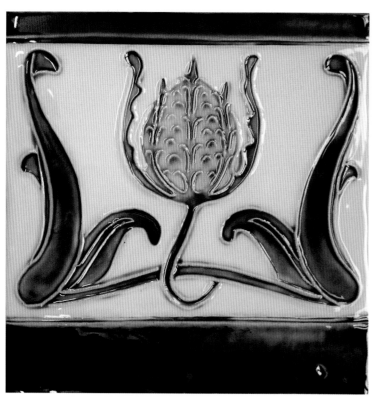

Screen printed plastic clay tile with a reproduction Victorian floral design. 6" square. 1990s. *Courtesy of Janet Steele.* Price group A.

Tube-lined plastic clay tile with a reproduction Victorian border design. 6" square. 1990s. *Courtesy of Janet Steele.* Price group A.

Hand painted plastic clay tile depicting a frog eyeing his dinner, designed and painted by Janet Steele for the author's wife. 150mm square. 1990s. *Courtesy of Julia Blanchett.* Price group A.

NORTON TILE COMPANY
The art of hand made tiles   Tel: 01243 544227

Examples of wildflowers painted on a cream glazed, dimpled 100mm tile. The panel below was one of two, a digital photo distorts the colour of the background glaze, it does in fact match those shown on insert tiles which were made to go with the panels.

£8 each painted 100mm dimpled faced hand crafted tiles.

Norton Tile Co. catalog page showing range of wild flower designs on 100mm plastic clay tiles.

Identification and Marks

Janet marks her hand painted panels with a monogram of her initials.

Painted mark. 1995- .

Philippa Threlfall
Black Dog of Wells

Tor Street, Wells, Somerset

Artist and designer Philippa Threlfall and her husband, the historian Kennedy Collings (b.1933-d.2002) were responsible for over a hundred major ceramic installations, mainly high relief murals in ceramic and concrete based on historical themes. These were produced in Britain and abroad from the early 1960s to the mid-1980s. Since then, the family business, Black Dog of Wells, has produced a range of small scale terra cotta plaques. These are sold under the Black Dog trade name through outlets such as National Trust properties throughout the U.K.

Unglazed relief molded terra cotta tile depicting a dodo. 4" diameter. c.1995. *Courtesy of Roger Hensman.* Price group A.

Unglazed relief molded terra cotta tile depicting Adam and Eve, "God the first garden made." 4" square. c.1995. *Courtesy of Roger Hensman.* Price group A.

Unglazed relief molded terra cotta tile depicting a fruit tree, "Only God can make a tree." 4" square. c.1995. Price group A.

Identification and Marks

Rubber-stamp mark used on card mount covering back of tile.

ness designing and screen printing tiles to commission from his home address in Poole, Dorset. These designs were produced in very small numbers and on a wide range of blanks sourced from *Maw & Co., Campbell Tiles Ltd., Carter & Co.* and others.

Reginald Till 1955-c.1957

31c Commercial Road, Parkstone, Poole, Dorset

Reginald Till was born in North Staffordshire and trained at Stoke School of Art and the Royal College of Art. In 1923, he joined *Carter & Co.* in Poole, Dorset and was responsible for a number of their tile designs. One of the special projects on which he worked was the design of tiles for the first class swimming pool of the *Queen Mary*. In 1948, Carter & Co. received a large, urgent order from Ethiopia for tiles, and Till suggested employing silk-screen printing to produce the order within the tight schedule available. The inspiration for this came from his part-time evening teaching at Poole School of Art, where he met Margaret Thomas who taught fabric design. His success with this early project led to Carter's experiments with automating silk-screen printing, which was first achieved in 1951. Till was responsible for some of the company's earliest screen printed series, including "Country Scenes" and "Pub Games." Disappointed with Carter's lack of acknowledgement of his involvement in this revolutionary process, he left the company in 1952 to join the newly formed *Purbeck Decorative Tile Co.* He stayed with them until 1955, when he set up his own small busi-

Photo litho transfer printed over-glaze tile depicting flowers. 4" square. c.1955. Campbell Tile Co. blank. Price group A.

Photo litho transfer printed over-glaze tile depicting flowers. 4" square. c.1955. Campbell Tile Co. blank. Price group A.

Photo litho transfer printed over-glaze tile depicting flowers. 4" square. c.1955. Maw & Co. blank. *Courtesy of the Ironbridge Gorge Museum Trust.* Price group A.

Photo litho transfer printed over-glaze tile depicting leaves. 4" square. c.1955. H . & E. Smith blank. Price group A.

Rubber-stamp mark on Carter and Co. 4" square blank.

Kenneth Townsend (b.1931-d.1999)
Kenneth Townsend Tiles c.1967-c.1980

57 St Mary's Terrace, Hastings, Sussex

Kenneth Townsend was a freelance artist and painter who created large canvases in bright, bold colors and also made tiles that he screen printed on commercial blanks bought in from *Carter & Co.* and *Hereford Tiles Ltd*. His initial experience of ceramics came from working with his brother Dennis, who operated the Iden Pottery in nearby Rye. His designs fall into

Hand screen printed over-glaze tile depicting a hedgehog, pattern no. 4 from the "Menagerie" series. 6" square. 1967. Candy & Co. blank. *Courtesy of Mary Bentley.* Price group B.

two series: "Menagerie" and "London Designs." The "Menagerie" series of twenty-five designs features wonderfully stylized wild and domesticated animals, whilst the "London Designs" series of five designs depicts stylized characters drawn from London life. He also designed a lion tile for the Longleat Gallery, which was situated at the Longleat Safari Park in Wiltshire.

Hand screen printed over-glaze tile depicting a hen (this design does not appear in Kenneth Townsend's 1979 catalog). 6" square. c.1968. Hereford Tiles blank. *Courtesy of Mary Bentley.* Price group B.

Hand screen printed over-glaze tile depicting a gorilla, pattern no. 13 from the "Menagerie" series. 6" square. c.1968. Hereford Tiles blank. *Courtesy of Mary Bentley.* Price group B.

Hand screen printed over-glaze tile depicting a ram, pattern no. 22 from the "Menagerie" series. 6" square. c.1968. Hereford Tiles blank. *Courtesy of Roger Hensman.* Price group B.

Hand screen printed over-glaze tile depicting "British Lion," pattern no. 25 from the "Menagerie" series. 6" square. c.1968. Hereford Tiles blank. *Courtesy of Roger Hensman.* Price group B.

Hand screen printed over-glaze tile depicting an owl, a variation or possibly an earlier version of pattern no. 3 from the "Menagerie" series. 6" square. c.1968. Hereford Tiles blank. *Courtesy of Mary Bentley.* Price group B.

Hand screen printed over-glaze tile depicting an owl, pattern no. 3 from the "Menagerie" series. 6" square in original frame. c.1970. Unknown commercial blank. *Courtesy of Adrian Grater.* Price group B.

Hand screen printed over-glaze tile depicting a pig, pattern no. 9 from the "Menagerie" series. 6" square. c.1968. Hereford Tiles blank. *Courtesy of Mary Bentley.* Price group B.

Three hand screen printed over-glaze tiles depicting a ram, pattern no. 22; a hedgehog, a variation or possibly an earlier version of pattern no. 23; and a pelican, pattern no. 17, all from the "Menagerie" series. Each tile 6" square. c.1968. Hereford Tiles blanks. *Courtesy of Mary Bentley.* Price group B (each).

Hand screen printed over-glaze tile depicting a cow, pattern no. 10 from the "Menagerie" series. 6" square in original frame. c.1970. Unknown commercial blank. *Courtesy of Adrian Grater.* Price group B.

Hand screen printed over-glaze tile depicting a lion, pattern no. 16 from the "Menagerie" series. 6" square. 1971. Carter & Co. blank. Price group B.

Hand screen printed over-glaze tile depicting a tiger, pattern no. 8 from the "Menagerie" series. 6" square. 1971. Carter & Co. blank. Price group B.

Hand screen printed over-glaze tile depicting a donkey, pattern no. 12 from the "Menagerie" series. 6" square. 1972. Carter & Co. blank. Price group B.

Hand screen printed over-glaze tile depicting a robin, pattern no. 14 from the "Menagerie" series. 6" square. c.1974. Pilkington's + Carter blank. Price group B.

Hand screen printed over-glaze tile depicting a hen, pattern no. 2 from the "Menagerie" series. 6" square. c.1974. Pilkington's + Carter blank. *Courtesy of Mary Bentley.* Price group B.

Hand screen printed over-glaze tile depicting a "City Gent," pattern no. 26 from the "London Designs" series. 6" square. 1975. Pilkington's + Carter blank. Price group B.

Hand screen printed over-glaze tile depicting "Chelsea Pensioners," pattern no. 27 from the "London Designs" series. 6" square. 1975. Pilkington's + Carter blank. Price group B.

Hand screen printed over-glaze tile depicting a "Lifeguard," pattern no. 28 from the "London Designs" series. 6" square. 1970. Carter & Co. blank. Price group B.

Hand screen printed over-glaze tile depicting a "Beefeater,"
pattern no. 29 from the "London Designs" series. 6" square. 1970.
Carter & Co. blank. Price group B.

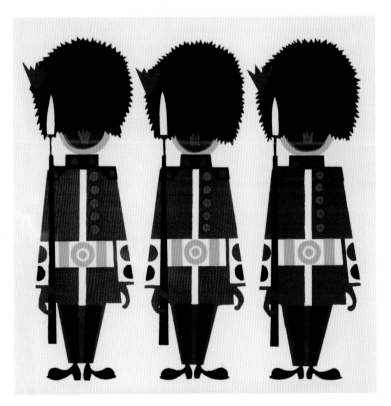

Hand screen printed over-glaze tile
depicting "Grenadier Guards," pattern no.
30 from the "London Designs" series. 6"
square. 1974. Pilkington's + Carter blank.
Courtesy of Mary Bentley. Price group B.

Rubber-stamp mark on Hereford Tiles 6" square blank, c.1967-c.1970. *Courtesy of Mary Bentley.*

Rubber-stamp mark on Pilkington's Tiles 6" square blank, c.1970-c.1984.

Troika Pottery 1963-1983

1963-1970: The Wells Pottery, St Ives, Cornwall
1970-1983: Newlyn, Cornwall

In February 1963, Leslie Illsley, Jan Thompson, and Benny Sirota each put up £1,000 and purchased the lease of the Wells Pottery at St Ives, Cornwall. Benny Sirota was the only potter of the three; Illsley was a sculptor and Thompson an architect. At first they could only make small items including tiles, due to the size of their kiln. But after a short time they purchased a larger kiln and started making pots and vessels. Jan Thompson left the company in 1966 and moved to Scandinavia. In 1970, the lease on their premises expired and because the local council refused to renew it, Leslie and Benny moved to new premises seven miles away at Newlyn, Cornwall, where they continued until the pottery closed in 1983.

The ultra modern design of their pottery took some time to catch on but when it was marketed at a number of major stores in London their style began to be accepted. Their tiles are distinctively dark and rough textured, being made from a modified stoneware decorated with dark oxides and a dull glaze.

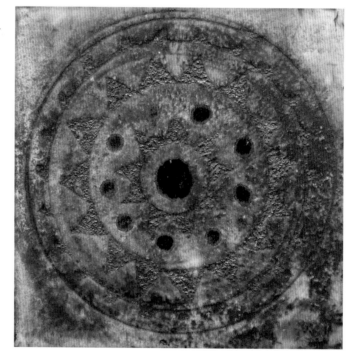

Hand painted and sgraffito stoneware tile with a geometric design. 6" square. c.1970. *Courtesy of Roger Hensman.* Price group B.

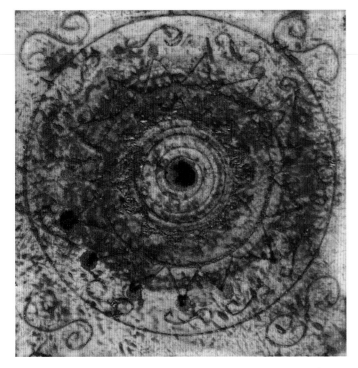

Hand painted and sgraffito stoneware tile with a geometric design. 6″ square. c.1970. *Courtesy of Roger Hensman.* Price group B.

Painted mark used on the back of plastic clay tiles. *Courtesy of Roger Hensman.*

Joanna Veevers 1992-

38 Cicada Road, London SW18

Trained initially as a textile designer, Joanna Veevers subsequently studied ceramics at the Royal College of Art, graduating with an MA in 1985. In 1986, she was awarded a Crafts Council setting-up grant and established her studio in Wandsworth, South London. In 1989, she was awarded first prize for design from the INAX Corporation in Japan, where she worked for three months, designing tiles for commercial production. She has undertaken a number of prestigious commissions, including ceramic wall pieces and drawings for Lewisham Hospital, London in 1992. A set of nine tiles designed and made in 1994 are on display at Nottingham Castle Museum and Art Gallery.

Joanna creates slip-cast semi-porcelain tiles decorated with stained slips. The slips are drawn on smooth plaster slabs using painting and drawing techniques. The tiles are then cast over the design, causing the stained slips to be picked up from the plaster mold as the clay dries. The tiles are then fired to 1200°C.

Hand decorated slip cast semi-porcelain tile depicting toy ships. 200mm square. 1990s. *Courtesy of and photograph by Joanna Veevers.* Price group C.

Identification and Marks

Joanna Veevers signs her tiles on the front with her initials or full signature.

Jonathan Waights
Art on Tiles 1984-

1984: 101 Farm Lane, Fulham, London, SW6 (with Paul Henry, Purbeck Decorative Tiles)

1984-1991: Unit 203 Wandsworth Workshops, Wandsworth, London, SW18

1991: The Old Gasworks, Wandsworth, London, SW18 (with Paul Henry again)

1992-1995: Ceramic Tile Design, 56 Dawes Road, Fulham, London, SW6 (with Chris Crew-Reed)

1995-1999: 8 Royal Parade, Fulham, London, SW6

1999-2002: The William Booker Yard, The Street, Walberton, West Sussex.

2002- : 2 Orchard Terrace, Walberton, West Sussex

Jonathan Waights was first introduced to tiles at the age of eighteen on a beach in Portugal. He was talking with a friend whose family was in the wine trade and had begun to make ceramic wine bottles. The family owned a number of historic buildings, several of which had tiles that were in need of replacement, and Jonathan was recruited to the ceramic bottle division to re-create the traditional Portuguese azulejos (tin-glazed tiles). On his return to Britain shortly after, Jonathan established Art on Tiles to produce traditional tin-glazed and other types of tile.

In the early days, Jonathan rented space in the workshop used by Paul Henry for his company *Purbeck Decorative Tiles* and Paul gave Jonathan the help and encouragement he needed to get established. Over the next fifteen years, Art on Tiles moved workshops a number of times, but always within the Wandsworth and Fulham areas of London. Then in 1999, the business moved to Walberton, a small village near Arundel in West Sussex, where Jonathan continues to produce tiles and tile panels in various techniques.

Jonathan creates most of his own designs, drawing upon and freely adapting traditional motifs and designs, both from tiles and other decorative sources. He works in under-glaze, in-glaze, and over-glaze techniques, using biscuit tiles purchased from *H. & R. Johnson Ltd.*, *H. & E. Smith Ltd.*, Paris Ceramics (imported), and *Clayworth Potteries*. The tiles are fired in a small, conventional electric kiln at varying temperatures to suit the nature of the glazes and work.

Panel of twelve hand painted tiles depicting irises within a border. Each large tile 6" square in original wooden frame. 1984. H. & R. Johnson blanks. *Courtesy of and photograph by Jonathan Waights.* Price group C (panel).

Panel of twelve hand painted tiles depicting jonquils within a border. Each large tile 6" square in original wooden frame. 1984. H. & R. Johnson blanks. *Courtesy of and photograph by Jonathan Waights.* Price group C (panel).

Photograph of display panel showing thirty-nine hand painted border tiles. Each tile 3" x 6". c. 1984. Unknown commercial blanks. *Courtesy of and photograph by Jonathan Waights.* Price group A (each tile).

Panel of twenty-four hand painted tiles depicting a Buddhist deity. Each large tile 6" square in original wooden frame. 1984. H. & R. Johnson blanks. *Courtesy of and photograph by Jonathan Waights.* Price group D (panel).

Panel of thirty hand painted tiles depicting an underwater scene within a border. Each large tile 6" square.
1985. H. & R. Johnson blanks. *Courtesy of and photograph by Jonathan Waights.* Price group D (panel).

Panel of thirty hand painted over-glaze tiles depicting a traditional delftware "Bloempot" design within a border. Each large tile 8" square. 1988. H. & R. Johnson blanks. *Courtesy of and photograph by Jonathan Waights.* Price group E (panel).

Panel of thirty-five hand painted tiles depicting a traditional Portuguese portrayal of Poseidon within a border. Each tile 5" square. c.1995. Imported rustic blanks from Paris Ceramics, London. *Courtesy of and photograph by Jonathan Waights.* Price group E (panel).

Panel of forty-two hand painted tiles depicting a traditional delftware polychrome "Bloempot" design within a border. Each large tile 6" square. c.1988. H. & R. Johnson blanks. *Courtesy of and photograph by Jonathan Waights.* Price group E (panel).

Panel of forty-two hand painted over- and under-glaze tiles with additional sponging and spraying, depicting a scene from the ceiling of the Sistine Chapel by Michaelangelo.. Each large tile 6" square. c.1997. H. & R. Johnson blanks. *Courtesy of and photograph by Jonathan Waights.* Price group E (panel).

Panel of thirty-six hand painted over- and under-glaze tiles depicting a nude Psyche in the style of Lord Leighton. Each tile 6" square. c.1995. H. & R. Johnson blanks. *Courtesy of and photograph by Jonathan Waights.* Price group E (panel).

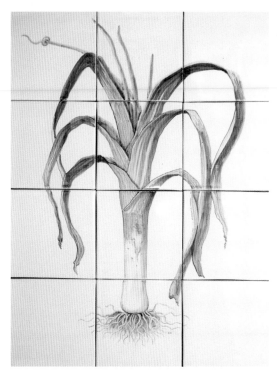

Panel of twelve hand painted tiles depicting a leek. Each tile 6" square. c.1999. Clayworth blanks. *Courtesy of Jonathan Waights.* Price group D (panel).

Panel of forty-two hand painted tiles depicting a scene from the Bayeaux Tapestry. Each tile 4" square. c.1999. Clayworth blanks. *Courtesy of and photograph by Jonathan Waights.* Price group E (panel).

Identification and Marks

Jonathan Waights signs most of his tile panels in full with "Jonathan Waights" or "J. Waights," sometimes with the addition of the last two digits of the year.

Alan Wallwork
Alan Wallwork Ceramics 1959-2004

1959-1964: Greenwich Studios, 19 Blackheath Road, London, SE10
1964-1989: Studios, Burton Street, Marnhull, Dorset
1989- 2004: Whitty Down Farm, Higher Rocombe, Uplyme, Lyme Regis, Dorset (not tiles)

Alan Wallwork's interest in ceramics commenced when he was undertaking a course at Goldsmith's College, London, where one of his tutors was *Kenneth Clark*. Although primarily a potter, Alan decorated a number of tiles from about 1959 to 1987 using an unusual technique of applying fluid glazes by slip-trailing onto a tile placed on a turntable. The glazes were then manipulated by wiping with a finger. These glazes were applied over commercial white glazed blanks supplied by *Pilkington's Tiles Ltd.* and *H. & R. Johnson Ltd.* The tiles were fired at approximately 1100ºC.

Alan's designs consisted of a range of five patterns, each supplied in a mix of colors from a standard range: golden yellow, amber, brown, olive green, and blue-green. He also produced a small number of tile-topped tables with fish designs.

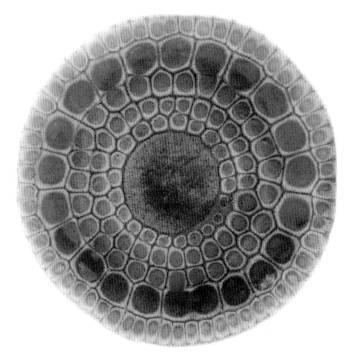

Hand painted glaze effect tile with an abstract design. 6" square. 1967. Pilkington's Tiles blank. Price group B.

Hand painted glaze effect tile with an abstract design. 6" diameter. c.1968.
H. & R. Johnson blank. Price group B.

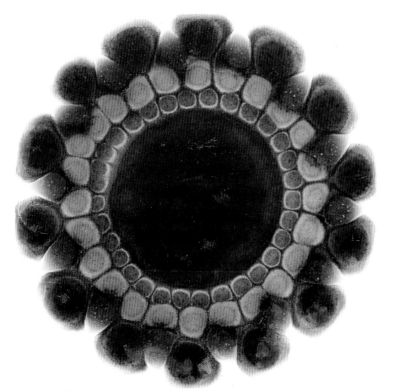

Hand painted glaze effect tile with an abstract design. 6"
square. c.1967. Pilkington's Tiles blank. Price group B.

Hand painted glaze effect tile with an abstract design. 6″ square. 1966.
Pilkington's Tiles blank. Price group B.

Hand painted glaze effect tile with an abstract design. 6″ diameter. c.1968.
H. & R. Johnson blank. Price group B.

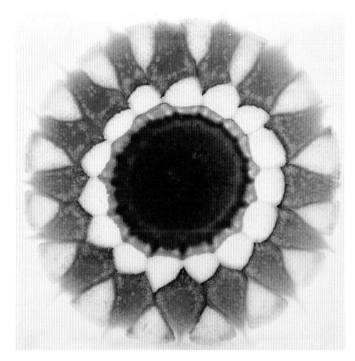

Hand painted glaze effect tile with an abstract design. 4¼″ square. 1967.
Pilkington's Tiles blank. Price group B.

Hand painted glaze effect tile with an abstract design. 6″ square. 1967.
Pilkington's Tiles blank. Price group B.

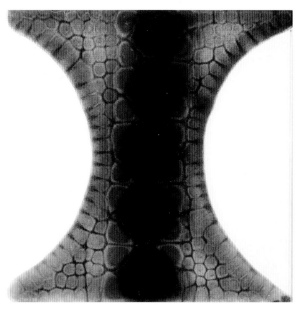

Hand painted glaze effect tile with an abstract design. 6″ square. 1967. Pilkington's Tiles blank. Price group B.

Hand painted glaze effect tile with an abstract design. 6″ square. c.1968. Pilkington's Tiles blank. Price group B.

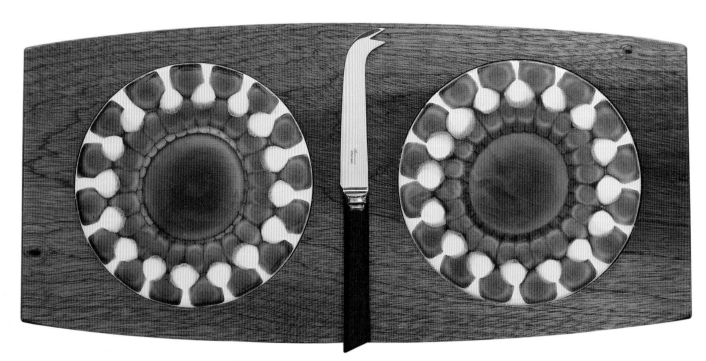

Cheese board inset with two hand painted glaze effect tiles with an abstract design. Each tile 6″ diameter. c.1967. H. & R. Johnson blanks. Price group B.

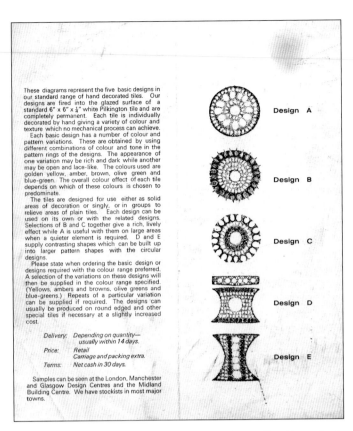

These diagrams represent the five basic designs in our standard range of hand decorated tiles. Our designs are fired into the glazed surface of a standard 6" x 6" x ¼" white Pilkington tile and are completely permanent. Each tile is individually decorated by hand giving a variety of colour and texture which no mechanical process can achieve.

Each basic design has a number of colour and pattern variations. These are obtained by using different combinations of colour and tone in the pattern rings of the designs. The appearance of one variation may be rich and dark while another may be open and lace-like. The colours used are golden yellow, amber, brown, olive green and blue-green. The overall colour effect of each tile depends on which of these colours is chosen to predominate.

The tiles are designed for use either as solid areas of decoration or singly, or in groups to relieve areas of plain tiles. Each design can be used on its own or with the related designs. Selections of B and C together give a rich, lively effect while A is useful with them on large areas when a quieter element is required. D and E supply contrasting shapes which can be built up into larger pattern shapes with the circular designs.

Please state when ordering the basic design or designs required with the colour range preferred. A selection of the variations on these designs will then be supplied in the colour range specified. (Yellows, ambers and browns, olive greens and blue-greens.) Repeats of a particular variation can be supplied if required. The designs can usually be produced on round edged and other special tiles if necessary at a slightly increased cost.

Delivery: Depending on quantity— usually within 14 days.
Price: Retail Carriage and packing extra.
Terms: Net cash in 30 days.

Samples can be seen at the London, Manchester and Glasgow Design Centres and the Midland Building Centre. We have stockists in most major towns.

Design A

Design B

Design C

Design D

Design E

A Greenwich Studios Ceramics leaflet showing Alan Wallwork's standard tile designs c.1967.

Rubber-stamp mark on H. & R. Johnson 6" diameter blank. 1964-1989 (used on old stock sold from the Marnhull Studio).

Identification and Marks

Rubber-stamp mark on Pilkington's Tiles 6" square blank. 1959-1964 (contemporary with decoration).

Rubber-stamp mark on Pilkington's Tiles 6" square blank. 1989-2005 (used on old stock sold from the Uplyme Studio).

References

Wallwork, Alan. *Greenwich Studios Ceramics, Alan Wallwork.* Studio leaflet c.1960.

Sarah Walton 1978-

Keeper's, Bo-Peep Lane, Alciston, Nr Polegate, East Sussex

Sarah Walton is one of very few producers of salt-glazed tiles in the U.K. Her inspiration comes from an appreciation of the way surfaces are eroded over hundreds of years by the effects of use and weathering. The stoneware clay she uses produces an extremely hard and durable tile although, because of the high firing temperature, some warping is inevitable. This, however, contributes a three dimensional feel and tactile richness to the final surface. The coloring of the tiles is similar to that of English medieval tiles from the 12th to 15th centuries, namely earth colorings ranging through gray, cream, pink, orange, and red to rich dark brown.

Most of her tiles are plain but she has also introduced some linear patterns and occasional decorative motifs featuring bowls of fruit, fish, Thames barges, and trees into her range. These are impressed into the surface at the plastic clay stage before firing to 1280°C alongside her plain tiles. The tiles are produced in two sizes, nominally 4½" and 6" square, and are formed by press molding in a wooden mold. At the leather hard stage, a colored slip is applied to the surface to give the finished color. The tiles are arranged in the kiln on edge in zigzag rows, each layer being held upright by the weight of the shelf above. At the highest temperature point of the firing, salt is introduced into the kiln; this vaporizes and forms a natural glaze in reaction with the surface of the clay.

Incised salt-glazed stoneware tile depicting a Thames sailing barge. 4-3/8" square. c.1990. *Courtesy of Eric James Mellon.* Price group B.

Identification and Marks
No identifying marks.

Nicola Werner
Nicola Werner Majolica Pottery & Tiles 1986-

1986-1987: Trottiscliffe, Kent
1987-1992: Milverton, Somerset
1992-1998: Hemyock, Somerset
1998- : Burcombe Farm, Bolham Water, Clayhidon, Nr
Cullompton, Devon

Born in 1959, Nicola Werner was brought up in rural Kent and attended the foundation course at Medway College of Art & Design. She then studied fine art (painting) at the Central School of Art in London. After a year, she left and took up ceramics in a bid to make "practical art" and a living. For three years starting in 1983, she worked with *Alan Caiger-Smith* at his Aldermaston Pottery in Berkshire. This experience proved invaluable to her and in 1986, after some months researching designs and painting watercolors in the Lake District, she set up her own pottery in Trottiscliffe, Kent.

Nicola produces a wide range of domestic wares, one-off commemorative pieces, and an increasing variety of tiles including murals to commission, as well as a standard range. In 1992, she produced a limited edition of commemorative tiles for Queen Elizabeth II Golden Jubilee and in 1994 a range of six special designs for the Victoria & Albert Museum. She decorates biscuit tiles purchased from *H. & E. Smith Ltd.* and *H. & R. Johnson Ltd.*; these are dipped in tin-glaze and then hand painted. The tiles are fired alongside her pots to 1060°C.

Hand painted tin glaze tile depicting a hen. 6" square. c.1990. H. & R. Johnson blank. *Courtesy of Roger Hensman.* Price group A.

Identification and Marks

Painted initials mark with additional mark for year.

Bronwyn Williams-Ellis 1975-

Old Orchard, 88a Walcot Street, Bath, Avon

Born in Burton-on-Trent in Staffordshire, Bronwyn Williams-Ellis is the niece of Clough Williams-Ellis, the famous Welsh architect whose tour-de-force was the fairy-tale village of Portmerion in North Wales. Bronwyn, however, has forged a personal career in making architectural and sculptural ceramics and tiles, starting with a number of commissions for tiles and panels for Portmerion itself. Since then, she has produced a wide range of designs mainly to commission, and has designed a range of tiles and small panels for *Fired Earth*.

Originally, Bronwyn worked on commercial blanks, but she now concentrates on her own hand-made biscuit except for some large commissions. Her tiles are hand painted and modernist in style, reflecting a strong sense of line and pattern. Themes include people swimming, birds in flight, and especially things of the sea: shells, mermen etc. Originally, Bronwyn used highly alkaline glazes similar to those used on old Russian and Islamic tiles, giving bold definition and a glossy finish, but in recent years she has moved towards more earthy colors and rich terra cottas. Like her uncle before her, she is fascinated by the impact of intense color.

Twelve hand painted tin-glaze tiles depicting "Garden Tools." Each tile 6" square. 1990s. Unknown commercial blanks. *Courtesy of and photograph by Bronwyn Williams-Ellis.* Price group A (each tile).

Detail of a large panel of cuerda seca tiles, "Fish and Waves." Each tile 6" square. 1990s. Unknown commercial blanks. These tiles incorporate alkaline and tinglazes and are highlighted with platinum luster. *Courtesy of and photograph by Bronwyn Williams-Ellis.* Price group F (complete panel).

Selection of stenciled slip and alkaline glaze tiles in various designs and sizes. 6", 4", 2", and 1" square. 1990s. *Courtesy of and photograph by Bronwyn Williams-Ellis.* Price group A/B (each tile).

Selection of stenciled slip and fritted lead glaze tiles in various designs. Each tile 4" square. 1990s. *Courtesy of and photograph by Bronwyn Williams-Ellis.* Price group B (each tile).

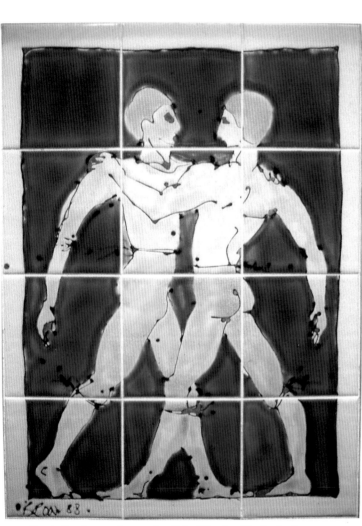

Panel of three hand made tiles depicting "Pattern of Movement." Overall size approximately 250mm x 1090mm. 1998. These tiles were made from an earthenware body, grogged white clay slips, and cuerda seca outlines. *Courtesy of and photograph by Bronwyn Williams-Ellis.* Price group E (panel).

Panel of twelve cuerda seca tiles, "The Wrestlers." Each tile 6" square. 1988. H. & R. Johnson blanks. *Courtesy of and photograph by Bronwyn Williams-Ellis.* Price group F (panel).

Panel of twelve hand made tiles depicting a "Diver." Overall size approximately 26" x 72". 1990s. These tiles were made from an earthenware sagger marl using oxide slips, a cuerda seca outline, and an alkaline glaze. *Courtesy of and photograph by Bronwyn Williams-Ellis.* Price group F (panel).

Panel of two hand made tiles depicting "Diver on Blue." Overall size approximately 24" x 9". 1995. These tiles were made from an earthenware body, cobalt slip, and a cuerda seca outline. *Courtesy of and photograph by Bronwyn Williams-Ellis.* Price group E (panel).

Identification and Marks
Some early tiles and panels are signed "BRON" with the last two digits of the year.

Mary Wondrausch
Mary Wondrausch Pottery c.1984-

The Pottery, Brickfields, Compton, Near Guildford, Surrey

Mary Wonrausch's initial interest in pottery was influenced by continental peasant art, but since the mid-1980s she has developed an overwhelming passion for English 16th century slipware. All her pots and tiles are made from local Fremington clay and slip-trailed with Bideford (Devon) pipe clay. She uses nine different slip-trailers of her own design with oxide-stained clays that are applied at the leather hard stage. After further drying, the tiles are biscuit fired at 980ºC and then clear glazed and glost fired to 1040ºC. Mary's work is meticulously detailed and a worthy tribute to the potters who created the early slipware some four hundred years ago.

Slip trailed tile depicting a hen. Approximately 6" square. 1990. *Courtesy of Thelma Shepley.* Price group B.

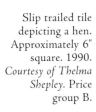

Slip trailed tile depicting a hen. Approximately 6" square. 1990. *Courtesy of Thelma Shepley.* Price group B.

Identification and Marks
No identifying marks.

Royce Wood & Peter Wood
Royce Wood Potters 1985-1997
Royce Wood Tiles Ltd. 1997-

1985-1987: Business Centre, Adams Close, Heanor, Derbyshire
1987-1989: Park Hall Craft Centre, Denby, Derbyshire
1990- : Holly Lane, Tansley, Matlock, Derbyshire

Royce Wood Potters began making fine art ceramics in 1985, when the company produced a collection of figurines and Toby jugs for historical sites in the U.K. such as the Tower of London, Hampton Court Palace, and Westminster Abbey. The studio was started as a partnership between painter and sculptor Royce Wood and her son, Peter Wood, on completion of his BA at The University of Hull. Royce Wood had completed her NDD at Derby College of Art after five years study, having been accepted at the age of fourteen on the strength of her work. She specializes in original sculptures and hand painting, producing work of outstanding quality and detail.

The company's first tile collection was unveiled at Expotile '97 to critical acclaim and featured a range of variegated glazed, relief molded tiles. Royce Wood created the figurative designs, including "Seashore," "Farm Animals," "Wildlife," "Art Nouveau," and "Fossils" series, and is also responsible for hand painted panels. The tiles are press molded and glazed with rich, lustrous glazes developed by Peter, and fired at 1150ºC in electric kilns. Peter is also responsible for the contemporary design collections and the growth and development of the business.

Royce's daughter, Angela, works in the family business too and has recently become a Director of the studio. Her areas of specialization include organization of the production facility and implementing business strategy. The studio now distributes its tiles through specialist tile retailers in the U.K. Recent designs have included "Geometric," "Retro," and "Gaudi" tiles and it is the desire to create individual, original, and unique designs that have made the business so successful.

Relief molded plastic clay tile, "Art Nouveau Honeysuckle on Mirage." 4" square. 1990s. Price group A.

Relief molded plastic clay tile, "Art Nouveau Anemone on Mirage." 4" square. 1990s. Price group A.

Hand decorated plastic clay tile, "Cube on Ecru." 4" square. 1990s. Price group A.

Hand decorated plastic clay tile, "Salsa Cube on Gold." 4" square. 1990s. Price group A.

Intaglio molded plastic clay tile, "Dragonfly on Sand." 4" square. 1990s. Price group A.

Hand decorated plastic clay tile, "Salsa Tri Colour on Gold." 4" square. 1990s. Price group A.

Intaglio molded plastic clay tile, "Fossil Amphibian on Moss." 4" square. 1990s. Price group A.

Hand decorated plastic clay tile, "Strata on Wheat." 4" square. 1990s. Price group A.

Relief molded plastic clay tile, "Dinosaur on Autumn." 4" square. 1990s. Price group A.

Relief molded plastic clay tile, "Mushroom on White." 4" square. 1990s. Price group A.

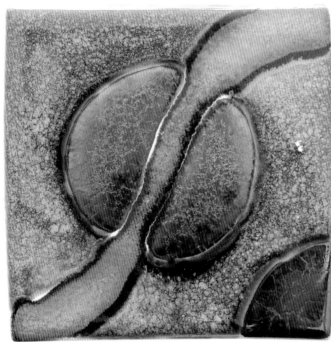

Hand decorated plastic clay tile, "Gaudi Planet." 4" square. 1990s. Price group A.

Relief molded plastic clay tile, "Orange on Moss." 4" square. 1990s. Price group A.

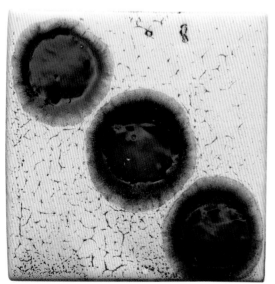

Hand decorated plastic clay tile, "Orbit on Crater." 4" square. 1990s. Price group A.

Relief molded plastic clay tile, "Scallop on Cascade." 4" square. 1990s. Price group A.

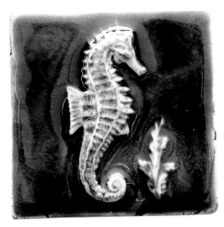

Relief molded plastic clay tile, "Seahorse on Largo." 4" square. 1990s. Price group A.

Relief molded plastic clay tile, "Starfish on Largo." 4" square. 1990s. Price group A.

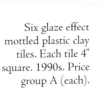

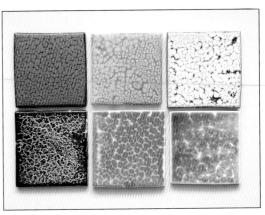

Six glaze effect mottled plastic clay tiles. Each tile 4" square. 1990s. Price group A (each).

Identification and Marks
No identifying marks.

Ymagynatyf Pottery 1920s

Chelsea, London

The Ymagynatyf Pottery was a small studio pottery established in the 1920s in fashionable Chelsea, London. They created mainly decorative pots and vases but also produced a very few decorated tiles, which appear to have been painted on *Minton Hollins* blanks. Examples of their tiles are particularly rare.

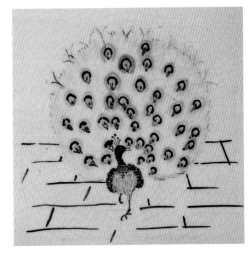

Hand painted tile depicting a peacock. 5" square. 1926. *Courtesy of Roger Hensman.* Price group B.

Identification and Marks

Hand-painted marks on Minton, Hollins and Co. 5" square blank. Dated "1926".

Bibliography

This bibliography encompasses general books on the subject of tiles and related materials. Books about individual companies etc. are found at the end of the relevant entry. Many of these books, and a wide range of others about tiles from around the world, are available from Buckland Books, 18 Woodlands Road, Littlehampton, West Sussex, BN17 5PP, U.K, Telephone: +44 (0) 1903 717 648, Fax: +44 (0) 1903 717 648, Email: buckland.books@tiscali.co.uk, Website: www.bucklandbooks.co.uk.

Artucio Urioste, Arq. Alejandro. *El Azulejo en la Arquitectura Uruguaya, Siglos XVIII, XIX, y XX.* Montevideo, Uruguay: Linardi y Risso, 2004. (Includes a large number of British tiles exported to Uruguay in the early 20th century.)

Austwick, J. & B. *The Decorated Tile.* London: Pitman House, 1980.

Barnard, Julian. *Victorian Ceramic Tiles.* London: Studio Vista/ Christies, 1972 & 1979.

Celoria, Francis, & Peter Clegg. *The Tile File.* Leeds: Tiles and Architectural Ceramics Society, 1998. (A listing of Victorian and 20th century tile manufacturers on CD ROM.)

Durbin, Lesley. *Architectural Tiles, Conservation and Restoration.* Amsterdam & London: Elsevier, Butterworth Heinemann, 2005.

(Exhibition Catalog). Van Lemmen, Hans, & John Malam (Editors). *Fired Earth, 1000 Years of Tiles in Europe.* Ilminster, Somerset: Richard Dennis Publications & Leeds: Tiles and Architectural Ceramics Society, 1991.

(Exhibition Catalog). *Condensing Time and Light into Ceramic: Old Tiles from Taiwan and the Netherlands.* Taipei, Taiwan: Taipei County Yingge Ceramics Museum, 2003. (Contains information on Japanese Art Nouveau tiles, many of which were copies of contemporary English tiles.)

Fowler, Sandie, & Wendy Harvey. *Art Nouveau Tiles c.1890-1914.* Atglen Pennsylvania: Schiffer Publishing Ltd., 2002.

Furnival, William J. *Leadless Decorative Tiles, Faïence and Mosaic.* Stone, Staffordshire: privately published by the author, 1904. (This is a fascinating book covering the history and manufacturer of decorative tiles. It was written as a diatribe against the needless death of pottery workers from lead poisoning and published at the author's expense. Although only 400 copies were printed, it was responsible for changing the law and making the pottery industry a much safer workplace.)

Graves, Alun. *Tiles and Tilework of Europe.* London: Victoria & Albert Museum, 2002.

Greene, John. *Brightening the Long Days, Hospital Tile Pictures.* Leeds: Tiles and Architectural Ceramics Society, 1987. (A detailed study of the use of tile panels in British hospitals from c.1880-1930).

Herbert, Tony, & Kathy Huggins. *The Decorative Tile in Architecture and Interiors.* London: Phaidon Press, 1995.

Johnson, Tony. *The Morris Ware, Tiles & Art Pottery of George Cartlidge.* Whippingham, Isle of Wight: MakingSpace, and the author, 2004.

Kamermans, Johan, & Hans van Lemmen (Editors). *Industrial Tiles, 1840-1940.* Otterlo, Netherlands: Nederlands Tegelmuseum, 2004.

Lang, Gordon (Editor). *1000 Tiles, 2000 years of Decorative Ceramics.* London: A. & C. Black, 2004.

Leboff, David. *The Underground Stations of Leslie Green.* Harrow, Middlesex: Capital Transport, 2002. (Has much information on the use of tiles on the London Underground from 1900 on.)

Lockett, Terence A. *Collecting Victorian Tiles.* Woodbridge, Suffolk: The Antique Collectors' Club, 1979.

Messenger, Michael. *Pottery and Tiles of the Severn Valley.* London: Remploy, 1979.

Pearson, Dr Lynn F. *A Gazetteer of Tile Sites in Britain.* Ilminster, Somerset: Richard Dennis Publications, 2005.

Swann, Michael. *Tile Image Gallery CD-ROM.* Derby: Swann Internet Services, 1998. (A CD-ROM of Victorian and 20th century tiles.)

Teutonico, Jeanne Marie (Editor). *Architectural Ceramics: Their History, Manufacture and Conservation.* London: James and James/English Heritage, 1996.

Van Lemmen, Hans. *Tiles, A Collector's Guide.* London: Souvenir Press, 1979.

Van Lemmen, Hans. *Tiles in Architecture.* London: Laurence King, 1993.

Van Lemmen, Hans, & Chris Blanchett. *20th Century Tiles, a Shire Album.* Princes Risborough, Buckinghamshire: Shire Publications, 1999.

Van Lemmen, Hans, & Bart Verbrugge. *Art Nouveau Tiles.* London: Laurence King, 1999.

Van Lemmen, Hans. *Victorian Tiles, a Shire Album.* Princes Risborough, Buckinghamshire: Shire Publications, 2000.

Index